AN INVENTORY
of

Federal Income
Transfer Programs

Fiscal Year 1977

by
William J. Lawrence
Chairman,

Department of Economics
Pace University
Graduate School of Business

&

Stephen Leeds

With Foreword by
Leonard M. Greene, President
The Institute for Socioeconomic Studies

THE INSTITUTE FOR SOCIOECONOMIC STUDIES

White Plains   New York

The Institute For Socioeconomic Studies
Airport Road, White Plains, New York 10604

TABLE OF CONTENTS

FOREWORD

Welfare reform has been debated publicly for many years. There is general agreement that the existing system of overlapping and often redundant programs, which contain inherent work disincentives and inefficiencies, requires improvement. Much attention has focused on an approach that would cash out existing programs and substitute a single, federally financed income support program.

It is very difficult to discuss the possibilities for reform without a good understanding of the programs now in existence. Unfortunately, comprehensive knowledge of the existing system has been lacking.

In order to fill this gap, The Institute for Socioeconomic Studies has sponsored a comprehensive inventory of all governmental—Federal, state and local—income transfer programs. The work is being compiled under the direction of Dr. William J. Lawrence, chairman of the Department of Economics, Pace University Graduate School of Business. This volume marks the completion of the first phase of the investigation — the inventory of *all* Federal income transfers that aim to support or supplement an individual's current standard of living.

The Administration has recently proposed a Federal income support program that would cash out $28 billion of existing income transfers. While this is a step in the right direction, it represents a very small portion of existing Federal income transfers. The accompanying Federal inventory includes 182 programs accounting for an annual expenditure of $250 billion in Fiscal 1977. Thus, for every dollar collected by the Federal government as tax receipts, it gave out 69 cents in either direct or indirect benefits. While it may not be possible to cash out all of these programs in favor of a single new program, many could be consolidated.

It should be noted that this is the most comprehensive Federal inventory compiled to date. The most complete survey previously published was that of the Joint Economic Committee. It identified 102 Federal benefits programs. It is the hope of The Institute for Socioeconomic Studies that this comprehensive inventory will provide a better understanding of the scope of income transfers today and that it will lead in the future to the development of a system of greater equity, simplicity and coherence.

Leonard M. Greene
President
The Institute for Socioeconomic Studies

White Plains, New York
March, 1978

ACKNOWLEDGMENTS

This report results from the first phase of an ongoing effort to develop a comprehensive inventory of those Federal, state and local income transfer programs that provide individuals with cash and other benefits to support their current standard of living. It is hoped that this compilation of Federal programs may prove to be a helpful reference document to officials and policy analysts concerned with rationalizing and simplifying the nation's income security system.

All too frequently, national welfare reform is examined within the narrow focus of public assistance, food stamps and Medicaid. Set out here are descriptions of scores of other programs that also support or supplement individual incomes. These descriptions are not meant to be exhaustive or definitive; their purpose is to provide the reader with a general understanding of each program's operation, cost and impact in fiscal year 1977. More detailed information about a particular program of interest may be obtained from the appropriate Federal sources.

This research is being supported by a grant from The Institute for Socioeconomic Studies. The authors are particularly grateful to Dr. Leonard M. Greene, president of The Institute, for his continuing enthusiasm, assistance and advice.

The authors are also indebted to members of the Department of Economics of the Pace University Graduate School of Business and to the following students who assisted in the research and preparation of this document: Linda Albertelli, Howard Goldsman, Stanley Shipley and Jacqueline Slivko. Professor J. Knickman of the New York University Graduate School of Public Administration was particularly helpful in the formulation of the tax expenditure sections of the report. John Shrawder had the assignment of abstracting the budget data as presented for each program.

This work would not have been possible were it not for the dozens of Federal officials who took the time to explain the funding and functioning of various programs. Many of them have reviewed the manuscript.

Companion documents, covering state and local income transfer programs, will be compiled over the coming year or so.

William J. Lawrence
Chairman
Department of Economics

Stephen Leeds
Policy Analyst

Pace University Graduate School of Business
New York, New York
March, 1978

INTRODUCTION
AND DESCRIPTION OF
FEDERAL LEVEL INVENTORY
OF INCOME TRANSFERS

It is difficult to see how the nation's welfare programs can be simplified and rationalized without a basic understanding of the myriad other programs also distributing benefits to various segments of the population. While many of these income transfer programs serve the lower-income population generally, others are beamed at special groups, such as farmers, veterans, Indians, disaster victims, the elderly or the disabled. To the extent that many of these programs provide benefits to middle- and upper-income individuals, one might question the necessity of such expenditures, postulating instead that less would be better spent if it were focused on those in greater need. Thus, while all such programs contribute, in varying degrees, to the alleviation of distress, no overriding theme or theory unifies them at present. A reference document that identifies and describes all these operations could serve as a useful tool for those officials and policy analysts involved in planning welfare reform.

This report identifies and describes almost two hundred programs, operating at the Federal level of government and providing any of five types of benefits to support or supplement an individual's current standard of living. Such benefits may be in the form of (1) direct cash payments; (2) tax relief, through a reduction in personal income tax liabilities; (3) in-kind, essential goods and services, either free or at reduced prices; and (4) credit and (5) insurance, at terms more favorable than those available in the private sector.

Project Scope

Previous attempts to identify and describe the nation's income transfer programs have been less than satisfactory for several reasons. Very little has been accomplished at the state and local level where significant program funds are raised and where the multiplicity of approaches does not permit facile classification. At the Federal level, many programs are small enough, or specialized enough, or so divorced from legislative authority, that they have escaped analysis and scrutiny. A number of such programs do not even appear as separate line items in the Federal Budget; their costs are lumped together with other expenditures. Many of the largest programs—those with well-organized constituencies like farmers, veterans, or the aged, and often with their own, very protective Congressional committees—have been deliberately excluded, time and again, from consideration in conjunction with "welfare" reform.

A confusing array of schemes and definitions is in use throughout the Federal bureaucracy to describe those income transfer programs which are variously referred to as comprising the nation's income maintenance, income security, public welfare or social welfare system.

A helpful but somewhat narrow definition is utilized in the *Budget of the United States Government* to delineate the "income security" function as "income support payments to families and individuals that do not in return require the performance of services by recipients, (including) retirement, disability and unemployment insurance, and food assistance." Even this somewhat restrictive approach accounts for $137 billion in expenditures, or 35 percent of the 1977 Budget. A companion document, *Special Analyses, Budget of the United States Government,* utilizes a broader interpretation of income security, including some health, housing and veterans' benefits ignored above. This approach encompasses over $170 billion in direct expenditures, while the text notes that "in addition, tax expenditures for income security are expected to result in lost revenues of over $20 billion in 1977."

The Joint Economic Committee of Congress, in its *Studies in Public Welfare,* listed 102 Federal programs that in 1972 provided "cash benefits and cash substitutes directly to individuals, even though some of these programs do not explicitly base assistance on the individual's actual need." The JEC study superficially examined only those state and local transfers analogous to the Federal ones it enumerated. Its own list of Federal programs could have been expanded upon, under somewhat different—but nonetheless acceptable—constraints. Of crucial significance is the fact that *Studies in Public Welfare* disregarded indirect payments (*i.e.,* tax expenditures) as well as credit and insurance benefits to individuals.

Introduction

The JEC effort has not been updated to reflect the many program additions, deletions and modifications which have occurred since 1972.

It is our goal to identify and describe all the elements of the national income transfer system presently in operation. To this end, the inventory is as inclusive as possible. Our definitional standards range from those programs traditionally considered to be part of the system, to programs of similar intent not always considered as part of the system, to somewhat dissimilar programs over which one could expect theoretically valid demurrals.

We began with the Federal programs for several reasons. Federal benefits are most immediately related to the issues of national welfare reform which are now confronting Congress and the Administration. Moreover, the Federal system to a large extent determines the form and substance of the state and local systems which are typically structured to conform to, fill the gaps between, or supplement the effects of Federal income transfer programs. Then again, the Federal programs are the logical starting point, since they are more adequately documented than those at other levels of government.

The identification of programs for inclusion in this report has been accomplished by means of a two-tier procedure, involving both a review of the literature and discussions with appropriate Federal officials and other experts. As programs were uncovered, their basic characteristics were gleaned from such documents as the *Budget of the United States Government, Catalog of Federal Domestic Assistance, Studies in Public Welfare, Federal Subsidy Programs* (Joint Economic Committee, October, 1974), *Tax Expenditures* (Senate Budget Committee, March, 1976), and various agency documents, guidelines and pamphlets. The inventory that follows briefly describes each program's objective, benefits, beneficiaries, administration, legislative authority and expenditures in fiscal year 1977, as abstracted from such sources.

We have defined public income transfer benefits as government-funded and -regulated assistance which serves to maintain or to supplement the current standard of living of individuals whose personal incomes and resources are inadequate, or who have suffered either a substantial reduction in income or increase in expenses, or who are at risk of any of the above. Generally, such benefits are provided to, or on behalf of, individuals from whom the government does not require a product, service or asset in return. And, generally, these individuals must prove their need (*e.g.,* through insufficient income and assets) and/or demonstrate certain qualifying characteristics (*e.g.,* old age, disability) categorically associated with need.

Public income transfer programs in this report provide benefits to individuals in various forms:

1. in direct cash payments, with or without restrictions on their use;
2. in indirect cash payments, by means of decreased personal tax liabilities resulting from income tax credits and from reductions in taxable income due to exclusions, exemptions and deductions;
3. in kind, through the direct provision, or indirect purchase, of essential goods and services (*i.e.,* food, clothing, shelter, medical care) not otherwise available, or at lower prices or fees than in the private sector;
4. in credit, by means of loan and/or loan guarantees not otherwise available, or at more favorable terms (*i.e.,* lower interest rates, longer maturities, smaller down payments) than in the private sector; and
5. in insurance, by means of policies and policy guarantees not otherwise available, or available at more favorable terms (*i.e.,* lower premiums, greater coverage) than in the private sector.

To further delimit the foregoing, for our purposes public income transfer benefits do *not* include:

1. government-funded grants or fellowships, not based on financial need, for advanced study and/or research in specified fields, or for participation in international exchange programs, since their primary aim is other than support for the beneficiary's standard of living;
2. government subsidies to business, or to individuals in their roles as producers, investors, and factor owners in the marketplace, if the overriding aim is to influence their economic behavior rather than to support or supplement their presently or potentially inadequate standard of living;
3. government-funded public services, facilities and projects which are accessible to, and for the general

benefit of, an entire community or segment thereof and which do not selectively confer discrete and measurable amounts of current income support upon needy individuals; and

4. government-funded protective or custodial services for wards of the state such as homeless children, juvenile offenders, prisoners, and mental incompetents.

Programs traditionally considered part of the income security system provide cash or in-kind benefits and fall within the above constraints. With a few exceptions, programs providing tax, credit and insurance benefits, in that order, are less likely to be considered in the income security context. An example of such nontraditional income transfer programs is disaster assistance in the form of either low-interest emergency loans to farmers or flood insurance for property owners, both of which can have the effect of supporting temporarily needy or at-risk individuals. Another example is economic opportunity assistance, which has the effect of setting up individuals in businesses with adequate incomes, whether by means of farm-ownership or operating loans to family farmers, or Small Business Administration loans to disadvantaged or handicapped persons who would not otherwise have access to credit or such incomes.

Substantial disagreement, or widespread ignorance, is to be found even in regard to many cash and in-kind programs. Not universally accepted as part of the income transfer system are those programs also serving as deferred compensation (*e.g.,* veterans' medical services) or production subsidies (*e.g.,* deficiency payments to stabilize farmers' incomes), those compensating otherwise unemployed individuals for work performed in the public sector (*e.g.,* public service employment), those that benefit the individual's income by improving his community's resources or economy (*e.g.,* economic development grants), and those not addressed to the individual's immediate living standard (*e.g.,* educational and training assistance).

All such programs are represented in the inventory which follows. Just as their inclusion is sure to engender some debate or controversy, so, too, should it broaden our horizons when we consider what directions and dimensions national welfare reform ought to take. That, in the final analysis, is what this report is all about.

How the Inventory Is Organized

The inventory contains 182 programs, each assigned its own page. (This figure is somewhat arbitrary, inasmuch as many programs could have been subdivided further and presented as functional components, thereby dramatically increasing the thickness of this report.)

The 182 programs are arranged in four broad sections:

I. Programs providing benefits to replace earnings lost due to the age, disability, death or other absence of the primary earner;

II. Programs providing benefits to supplement the earned income of the family;

III. Programs providing benefits to supplement the general income of the family;

IV. Programs providing benefits to improve the earnings potential of the individual.

This division has been accomplished with only a moderate amount of "forcing square pegs into round holes." However, the programs could have been arranged just as satisfactorily by target population or type of benefit, by whether or not they are based on financial need, or even alphabetically by the name of the administering agency. All such sequencing can be equally misleading to the general reader, since there is no overriding scheme determining the national income transfer network. For this reason, a rigorous internal organization of each of the four sections has been avoided. Programs with similar objectives and target populations tend to be near one another, regardless of their relative acceptability as elements of the income transfer system. We hope the reader will discover some thought-provoking juxtapositions. (There is an index at the back of the report to facilitate reference to specific programs.)

At the top of each page in the inventory is the program name, and underneath it is the Federal agency (or agencies) responsible for program administration. For any program reorganized in 1977, we have chosen to use the Federal agency name under which it appears in the proposed 1978 *Budget*.

The narrative paragraph on each page describes in general terms the program's objective, target population, benefits, administration and financing, numbers of people served, and relation

6

to individual need. In this context, "need" always refers to financial need. Program benefits said to be conditioned on need are provided only to individuals who are able to meet certain income and/or assets criteria for low income. Program benefits said to be conditioned *in part* on need are provided in relation to such criteria in only some specified instances, or in such a fashion that they also aid, but to a lesser degree, those who do not have low incomes. Program benefits said to be *not directly* conditioned on need are provided to individuals who are able to satisfy certain demographic requirements frequently related to low income. For program benefits said to be *not* conditioned on need, none of the above holds true.

Following each narrative paragraph is a space containing the letter "A," "B," or "C." This is a somewhat subjective code, based on the authors' cumulative experience, and used to designate the relative acceptability of the program (within the income transfer context) to government officials and to policy analysts. Programs marked "A" are usually found in the literature of welfare reform. Programs marked "B" are found in such literature less often and/or are the subject of some theoretical disagreement in that context. Programs marked "C" are rarely discussed in relation to welfare reform or even income transfers, and their inclusion in the inventory might be successfully challenged.

The "Authorization" section of each page presents the legislative and executive citations for the program.

The "Budget Code" and "Catalog Code" are reference source identifications for those who may wish to gather more information on programs. The Budget Code is the table number (or numbers) in the fiscal year 1978 *Budget Appendix* under which funding for the program may be found. We have used the 1978 identification since that *Budget* is more generally available and more up to date with regard to estimated 1977 expenditures. The Catalog Code is the program number (or numbers) under which additional details may be found in the *1977 Catalog of Federal Domestic Assistance.* Tax expenditures do not appear in either document, and several other programs do not appear in the *Catalog.* In such cases, "none" is entered as appropriate. (The reader who chooses to look up a program in these two documents should be wary of making comparisons between *Budget* and *Catalog* data, since they are likely to be widely divergent.)

At the bottom of each page, the estimated fiscal year 1977 expenditure is presented for the program. (Comments, where necessary, are provided underneath that figure.) "Expenditure" in this context means outlay, as used in the *Budget,* or revenue loss, in the case of tax relief programs. An outlay is the total of checks and cash disbursed during a fiscal year in carrying out a program; as such, it disregards whether the commitments for such disbursements were made in the present year or in the past, by contract or otherwise.

Federal accounting procedures for loan and insurance funds maintained within the *Budget* can produce "negative" outlays in a given year, if the value of a fund's disbursements is exceeded by its income or receipts from premiums, repayments, interest revenue, etc. Such negative expenditures are noted in the inventory, but the funded capital outlay (the value of assets acquired, such as loans, notes or property) is presented in the comments section as well.

Expenditure figures in the inventory include estimates of each program's direct Federal "overhead," *i.e.,* its share of administrative staff salaries and expenses, as well as the costs of operations, maintenance, construction, and similar program support. Typically, the Federal overhead is two or three percent for programs not operated by the Federal government itself but by other entities on the basis of project or formula grants. For programs with federally controlled field operations, the overhead is generally five to ten percent, depending on the scope and complexity of the undertaking.

Every effort has been made to eliminate double-counting where intra-budget transfers occur. The inventory includes the transferred amount under one or the other of the programs affected by such bookkeeping practices.

Finally, the reader must be warned that Federal fiscal affairs were during 1977 in such a state of flux, due to the changeover in Administrations and programs as well as the instability of the national economy, that there are frequently several divergent cost estimates in circulation for a given program.

Essentially, our estimation procedure involved four steps:

1. making a first-cut approximation based on the fiscal year 1977 column of the 1978 *Budget Appendix* in conjunction, when possible, with the *1976 Catalog of Federal Domestic Assistance;*

2. comparing such amounts to the appropriate line or lines in the 1977 mid-session budget review by the Office of Management and Budget;

3. discussing any substantial discrepancies between figures derived by the above two steps with appropriate Federal officials; and

4. resolving remaining inconsistencies, when possible, with the help of the *1977 Catalog of Federal Domestic Assistance.*

Draft copies of this report have been sent to all relevant Federal agencies for review. Substantive corrections and revisions suggested by the agencies have been incorporated in the following pages.

SUMMARY
OF FEDERAL LEVEL
INCOME TRANSFERS

Distribution of Programs in the Inventory

Estimated Federal outlays during fiscal year 1977, for the 182 income transfer programs in our inventory, total $248,155,000,000—or just under a quarter of a trillion dollars.

A relatively few programs in the Federal inventory account for many of these aggregate expenditures. The five major components of the national Social Security system (*i.e.,* retirement, survivors, and disability pensions, as well as Medicare hospital and medical benefits) account for two out of every five dollars compiled in the inventory. Social Security retirement benefits alone involve more than $50 billion in outlays for the year.

The presence of a relatively few, very large programs among the total 182 can distort statistical generalizations. Thus, while the arithmetical average outlay for programs in the inventory is $1.36 billion (*i.e.,* $248.155 billion ÷ 182 programs), the median is lower by a factor of ten, or $149 million. Examination of program outlays reveals that a third of the programs involve an annual expenditure of under $50 million, and two thirds, under $300 million. Only one program in five disburses more than a billion dollars yearly (see Table 1).

The total of $248 billion has not been inflated unnecessarily by inclusion of questionable income transfer programs in the inventory. Such programs—those classified in the "C" group, as previously explained—account for $7 billion altogether, or less than three percent of the inventory's total outlays.

Since the classification of programs into "A," "B," and "C" groups is a somewhat subjective convention of the authors, for use by the lay reader, we do not intend to belabor the scheme much beyond the descriptive statistics stated immediately below.

"A" programs, those usually considered part of the income security system and primarily providing cash or in-kind benefits, number 47 in the Federal inventory. Total annual outlays for these programs are estimated to be $170 billion, or two out of every three dollars listed in the inventory. There are 88 "B" programs which, while similar in their income security function to those in the "A" group, are less frequently considered in relation to welfare reform. These programs, which include most of the tax relief measures, as well as a large number providing in-kind benefits, account for $71 billion in outlays, or over a fourth of the annual total.

There are 47 "C" programs in the Federal inventory, and they are typically small, as their disproportionately low aggregate outlays would indicate. Most operations involving credit or insurance benefits fall within this group, as do many measures geared toward farmers, disaster victims and postsecondary education or training. Only one of these programs is in the billion-dollar range. Over half of

TABLE 1

Percentage Distribution of Federal Income Transfer Programs, by Annual Outlay in Fiscal Year 1977

Outlay $ (millions)	Distribution of Programs
0-49	30%
50-99	11
100-199	12
200-299	10
300-999	17
1,000-4,999	12
5,000 or more	8
	100%

Total Programs— 182

Total Outlays— $248,155 million

Average Outlay— $1,363 million

Median Outlay— $149 million

the nontraditional "C" programs involve outlays of less than $50 million annually, and only a fifth expend more than $200 million.

The 182 programs in the Federal inventory can be categorized by the form of benefit each provides, *i.e.*, cash, in-kind, tax relief, credit or insurance. However, 27 programs grant more than one kind of benefit:

Benefits Provided	Number of Programs
Cash and In-Kind	17
Cash and Other	7
Credit and In-Kind	3
Total	27

Almost half the programs providing both cash and in-kind assistance are geared toward students or trainees who typically receive a cash stipend coupled with specified services. The programs providing both cash and tax, credit or insurance benefits generally involve loans to one class of beneficiary and outright cash grants to another. The three remaining multi-benefit programs couple loans with management assistance services to incipient farmers and businessmen; in content such aid is similar to that provided by various manpower training operations.

Distribution of Benefits within Programs

For the purposes of analysis, we have categorized the 27 multi-benefit programs by their principal form of aid and added them to the single-benefit programs (see Table 2). Cash benefits account for proportionately twice as much (62%) of all Federal income transfer outlays as their relative program numbers (32%) would indicate. Conversely, in-kind benefits account for proportionately half as much (22%) as their relative program numbers (41%) would indicate. Tax relief outlays (*i.e.*, foregone tax revenues) reflect their program numbers, but the value of credit and insurance benefits is disproportionately low (11% of programs vs. 1% of outlays). One reason for the latter situation is to be found in the definition of "outlays" used in the *Budget* for loan and insurance funds, *i.e.*, the net of program disbursements less income or receipts from premiums, repayments, interest revenue, etc.

The Social Security system is well represented in both the

cash and in-kind categories, with retirement, survivors and disability payments comprising just over half of all cash outlays, and with Medicare hospital and supplementary medical benefits accounting for two fifths of all in-kind aid. In-kind benefits themselves can be subdivided into four groups: medical, housing, food and other. (The "other" classification includes educational, training and social services.) Two thirds of all outlays for in-kind benefits entail medical care of one type or another, including many small veterans health

TABLE 2

Distribution of Federal Income Transfer Programs and Annual Outlays, by Form of Benefit, Fiscal Year 1977

Form of Benefit	Programs		Outlays	
	Number	%	$ (millions)	%
Cash	59	32	153,778	62
In-Kind	75	42	57,106	23
Tax Relief	28	15	34,970	14
Credit or Insurance	20	11	2,301	1
Total	182	100%	$248,155	100%

programs. A sixth of in-kind outlays result in food and nutritional assistance; and just five percent, or $3 billion, of in-kind outlays constitute housing benefits of different kinds.

Distribution of Programs by Benefit Relationship

We can also examine the 182 Federal income transfer programs in terms of the extent to which the provision of benefits is conditioned on the financial situation of the beneficiaries (see Table 3). Less than a quarter (23%) of all Federal outlays are provided, even in part, to individuals who must demonstrate insufficient incomes and/or assets to qualify for such aid. Almost two thirds of all outlays involve benefits to individuals who merely have to exhibit certain characteristics (*e.g.,* old age, disability, residence in a poverty area) generally associated with lower incomes. Another 13 percent of income transfer outlays do not even require this much of a test; but

TABLE 3

Distribution of Federal Income Transfer Programs and Annual
Outlays, by Benefit Relationship to Financial Need, Fiscal Year 1977

Relationship of Benefit to Financial Need	Programs		Outlays	
	Number	%	$ (millions)	%
Conditioned on Need	41	23	41,036	17
Conditioned, in Part, on Need	39	21	14,470	6
Not Directly Conditioned on Need	71	39	159,386	64
Not Conditioned on Need	31	17	33,263	13
Total	182	100%	$248,155	100%

among this group, over half the programs belong to the nontraditional "C" classification.

The five major programs of the Social Security system all fall within the group with benefits not directly conditioned on financial need. However, even if we were to disregard the Social Security disbursements, the remaining programs in the category would still involve substantially greater aggregate outlays than any other group.

Over all, the pattern of benefit outlays varies considerably according to the extent to which aid is based on financial need (see Table 4). Programs with benefits based wholly or in part on a beneficiary's income disburse more than half (55%) of their assistance in the form of in-kind goods and services. Other programs, those that are not "income-tested," disburse almost all (84% to 94%) of their aid as cash, either directly through money payments or indirectly by means of tax relief. Among non-income-tested programs, those conditioned on a beneficiary's characteristics overwhelmingly provide direct cash assistance (mainly Social Security benefits), while those not conditioned at all on need provide mostly tax relief. Among the non-income-tested outlays for in-kind aid, medical care benefits constitute over 90 percent, but this figure is true for less than half of income-tested, in-kind outlays.

It is understandable that tax relief represents a greater share of those outlays for which the demonstration of a low income is not

14

Summary

required, inasmuch as individuals with low incomes are less likely to file tax returns and thus benefit from a reduced tax liability. It is less clear why in-kind aid represents the chief form of assistance where income is tested, although this correlation surely reflects at least some carryover from the prevailing English Poor Law approach of helping the needy in as unpalatable a fashion as possible in order to goad them into self-support.

TABLE 4

Percentage Distribution of Federal Income Transfer Outlays, in Fiscal Year 1977, by Form of Benefit and Relationship to Financial Need

Relationship of Benefit to Financial Need	Form of Benefit				
	Cash	In-Kind	Tax Relief	Credit or Insurance	Total Percent ($ millions)
Conditioned on Need	42%	55%	3%	Z	100% ($41,036)
Conditioned, in Part, on Need	35%	57%	4%	4%	100% ($14,470)
Not Directly Conditioned on Need	75%	16%	9%	Z	100% ($159,386)
Not Conditioned on Need	36%	1%	58%	5%	100% ($33,263)
All Programs	62%	23%	14%	1%	100% ($248,155)

Z: Less than 0.5%.

Distribution of Outlays by Program Rationale

The inventory is divided into four broad sections corresponding to the rationale behind each program's design (see Table 5). Most program outlays (70%) are designed to replace the lost earnings of aged, disabled, dead or otherwise absent breadwinners, and Social Security accounts for three fifths of these expenditures. Outlays to supplement the insufficient or interrupted earnings of working families account for 17 percent of disbursements, but outlays to supplement family income, generally, involve a disproportionately low eight percent. And, while a fifth of all programs in the inventory aim to improve the earnings potential of individuals, these efforts only expend five percent of the income transfer funds.

Each of the four sections of the inventory exhibits its own pattern of benefits and outlays (see Table 6). Close to three fourths of Federal outlays for the replacement of earnings lost due to age, disability or death of a breadwinner take the form of cash aid, and

TABLE 5

Distribution of Federal Income Transfer Programs and Annual Outlays, by Program Rationale, Fiscal Year 1977

Program Rationale	Programs		Outlays	
	Number	%	$ (millions)	%
To Replace Earnings Lost Due to Age, Disability, Death, etc.	64	35%	$174,054	70%
To Supplement the Earned Income of the Family	31	17%	41,287	17%
To Supplement the General Income of the Family	53	29%	20,432	8%
To Improve the Earnings Potential of the Individual	34	19%	12,382	5%
Total	182	100%	$248,155	100%

almost all the remaining quarter are in kind. Only a fifth of all such benefits are conditioned, wholly or in part, on the financial status of the aided.

Among programs designed to supplement the earnings of working families, half the aid takes the form of cash assistance, and half, tax relief. On the other hand, general supplementation of family

TABLE 6

Patterns of Benefit Outlay for Federal Income Transfer Programs, by Program Rationale, Fiscal Year 1977

| | Benefit Forms | | | | |
| | Primary | | Secondary | | |
Program Rationale	Form	% of Outlays	Form	% of Outlays	% of Outlays Conditioned Wholly or Partly on Need
To replace earnings lost due to age, disability, death, etc.	Cash	72%	In-Kind	23%	19%
To supplement the earned income of the family	Tax Relief	51%	Cash	49%	13%
To supplement the general income of the family	In-Kind	66%	Tax Relief	23%	64%
To improve the earnings potential of the individual	Cash	53%	In-Kind	33%	40%
All Programs	Cash	62%	In-Kind	23%	23%

income is accomplished primarily with in-kind aid (66%), with tax relief playing a decidedly secondary role (23%). While only 13 percent of outlays for earnings supplementation are based wholly or partly on financial need, this is true of 64 percent of outlays designed for general income supplementation.

Half the outlays designed to improve the earnings potential of individuals are in cash, and a third are in kind. Two fifths of all these outlays are income-tested.

In the pages that follow, the program descriptions themselves provide a more detailed overview of the Federal level income transfers presented above.

I
PROGRAMS PROVIDING BENEFITS TO REPLACE EARNINGS LOST DUE TO THE AGE, DISABILITY, DEATH OR OTHER ABSENCE OF THE PRIMARY EARNER

SUPPLEMENTAL SECURITY INCOME

Social Security Administration, Department of Health, Education & Welfare

Blind and disabled persons, as well as those age 65 or over, are provided direct monthly cash payments, if their adjusted incomes and resources fall below specified national standards. Payments are made to bring the beneficiary's total income up to the nationally established minimum; benefits are in the form of cash, without any restriction on its use. The established minimum monthly income for an individual is $168 and for a couple $252, if living alone; but many states pay additional sums above the federally financed national minimum. On the average, about 4.4 million recipients are aided monthly, and about half are aged. Benefits are conditioned on need.

A

Authorization: Title XVI, Parts A and B of the Social Security Act, as amended by PL92-603, PL93-66, PL93-233, PL93-368, PL94-566, PL94-569, and PL94-585.

Budget Code: 75-0406-0-1-604

Catalog Code: 13.807

FY77 Expenditure (est.)

$5,299 million

Excludes $1,515 million in state tax-levy supplementary payments.

EXCLUSION OF PUBLIC ASSISTANCE BENEFITS

Internal Revenue Service, Department of Treasury

Additional financial assistance is provided indirectly to individuals who receive any form of public assistance during the year. Benefits are in the form of tax relief, funded by allowing the recipient to exclude from consideration as income the value of such public aid. The exclusion covers cash assistance such as Aid to Families with Dependent Children and Supplemental Security Income. (Generally, fully dependent recipients would have no tax liability anyway, because of the low level of most public assistance payments. Those who benefit from this exclusion tend to be persons who are aided only for part of the year, or who are in families with other income sources.) Benefits are not directly conditioned on need.

B

Authorization: Revenue rulings under Section 61 of the Internal Revenue Code of 1954, as amended.

Budget Code: none

Catalog Code: none

FY77 Expenditure (est.)

$100 million

Represents estimated **FY77** revenue loss. About 93% of such tax expenditures go to tax filers with adjusted gross incomes under $7,000; and 7%, to those between $7,000 and $15,000.

AID TO THE AGED, BLIND AND DISABLED

Social and Rehabilitation Service, Department of Health, Education & Welfare

Public assistance to cover the minimum costs of food, shelter, clothing, and other items of daily living is provided to needy aged, blind and disabled adults in Guam, the Northern Marianas, Puerto Rico and the Virgin Islands. (U.S. territories and possessions did not participate in the changeover to the Supplemental Security Income program for such adults.) Benefits are directly paid to the needy adults in the form of cash, usually with no restrictions on its use, in monthly amounts varying according to each individual's countable income and needs, as determined under local law. Each month, on the average, 80,000 needy adults are aided in the U.S. territories and possessions. Benefits are conditioned on need.

A

Authorization: Social Security Act, as amended, 42 USC 1301 *et seq.,* 1351 *et seq.*

Budget Code: 75-0581-0-1-999

Catalog Code: 13.761

FY77 Expenditure (est.)

$5 million

Includes over 10% for local administration and other support.

ADDITIONAL EXEMPTION FOR THE BLIND

Internal Revenue Service, Department of Treasury

Indirect financial assistance is provided to blind taxpayers and to taxpayers with a blind spouse. Benefits are in the form of tax relief, funded by allowing the taxpayers to claim additional $750 personal exemptions from gross income. (This extra exemption is not applicable to other blind dependents.) The additional exemption is to compensate for the extra expense that a blind person has in order to live at a given standard. Benefits are not directly conditioned on need.

B

Authorization: Section 151(d) of the Internal Revenue Code of 1954, as amended.

Budget Code: none

Catalog Code: none

FY77 Expenditure (est.)

$20 million

Represents estimated FY77 revenue loss. About 27% of such tax expenditures go to tax filers with adjusted gross incomes under $7,000; and 40%, to those between $7,000 and $15,000.

ADDITIONAL EXEMPTION FOR THE AGED

Internal Revenue Service, Department of Treasury

Indirect financial assistance is provided to taxpayers who are 65 years of age, or older, and to taxpayers with a spouse of such age. Benefits are in the form of tax relief, funded by allowing the taxpayers to claim additional $750 personal exemptions from gross income. (This extra exemption is not applicable to other elderly dependents.) The additional exemption is to assist the elderly whose income sources are generally reduced by old age. Benefits are not directly conditioned on need.

B

Authorization: Section 151(c) of the Internal Revenue Code of 1954, as amended.

Budget Code: none

Catalog Code: none

FY77 Expenditure (est.)

$1,220 million

Represents estimated FY77 revenue loss. About 25% of such tax expenditures go to tax filers with adjusted gross incomes under $7,000; and 40%, to those between $7,000 and $15,000.

CREDIT FOR THE ELDERLY

Internal Revenue Service, Department of Treasury

Indirect financial assistance is provided to retired taxpayers who depend on income other than Social Security, Railroad Retirement, and similar tax-exempt payments. Benefits are in the form of tax relief, funded by allowing the retirees a credit of 15 percent of applicable income (up to certain limits) against tax liability. The credit is calculated upon the first $2,500 of non-tax-exempt income, including earnings, for single persons, and $3,750 for married couples. The base upon which the credit is calculated is reduced by any tax-exempt payments. The credit is phased out at adjusted income levels above $7,500 for single persons and $10,000 for married couples. Benefits are conditioned, in part, on need.

B

Authorization: Section 37 of the Internal Revenue Code of 1954, as amended by the Tax Reform Act of 1976.

Budget Code: none

Catalog Code: none

FY77 Expenditure (est.)

$495 million

Represents estimated FY77 revenue loss. Under former provisions, about 41% of such tax expenditures went to tax filers with adjusted gross incomes under $7,000; and 39%, to those between $7,000 and $15,000.

SPECIAL BENEFITS FOR PERSONS AGE 72 AND OVER

Social Security Administration, Department of Health, Education & Welfare

Retired persons who reached age 72 before 1968 (and their dependent or surviving spouses) are provided special monthly cash payments, even though the retired person did not work for a sufficient period of time to earn Social Security coverage. Benefits are directly paid to the beneficiary in the form of cash, without any restrictions on its use, in a monthly amount of $74 per person or $111 per couple. This program is funded by general revenue transfer payments into the Federal Old-Age and Survivors Insurance Trust Fund, and its purpose is to afford some protection to 180,000 persons who retired before the enactment of the Social Security Act or before their occupation was covered by the Act as amended. Benefits are conditioned on need, in part, since payments are reduced by the amount of most other government pensions, retirement benefits, and Supplemental Security Income.

A

Authorization: The Social Security Act, as amended by the Tax Adjustment Act of 1966, PL87-368; PL92-603; PL93-233, 42 USC 427-428.

Budget Code: 75-0404-0-1-999

Catalog Code: 13.804

FY77 Expenditure (est.)

$236 million

SOCIAL SECURITY — RETIREMENT INSURANCE

Social Security Administration
Department of Health, Education & Welfare

Retired workers over age 62 and their dependents are provided monthly cash payments, if the retired person has worked for a sufficient period of time to be insured, and the payments are made to replace income lost through retirement. Benefits are directly paid to the beneficiary in the form of cash, without any restriction on its use, in a monthly amount that ranges from $86 to $399 for retired individuals and from $162 to $704 for families. On the average, more than 17 million retired workers and 3.5 million of their dependents receive such benefits monthly. As social insurance, benefits are not directly conditioned on need as much as on past contributions by which the program is financed.

A

Authorization: Social Security Act as amended by PL92-603, PL93-66, PL93-233, 42 USC 401-429.

Budget Code: 20-8006-0-7-601

Catalog Code: 13.803

FY77 Expenditure (est.)

$52,364 million

EXCLUSION OF SOCIAL SECURITY BENEFITS

Internal Revenue Service, Department of Treasury

Additional financial assistance is provided indirectly to individuals who receive disability, retirement or survivors payments from Social Security. Benefits are in the form of tax relief, funded by allowing the beneficiaries to exclude from consideration as income those payments received from Social Security. Three fourths of this tax relief goes to elderly pensioners; the remainder is split between the disabled and the survivors. Benefits are not directly conditioned on need.

B

Authorization: IRS administrative rulings I.T. 3194 and I.T. 3229 (1939); I.T. 3447 (1941); and *Helvering vs. Davis,* 301 U.S. 619, 640.

Budget Code: none

Catalog Code: none

FY77 Expenditure (est.)

$4,240 million

Represents estimated FY77 revenue loss. About 52% of such tax expenditures go to tax filers with adjusted gross incomes under $7,000; and 32%, to those between $7,000 and $15,000.

RAILROAD RETIREMENT INSURANCE

Railroad Retirement Board

Railroad workers who retire at age 62 with at least 10 years of railroad employment, at age 60 with at least 30 years of service, and their dependent spouses, are provided monthly cash payments to replace income lost through retirement. Such payments may consist of from two to six components: Social Security benefits, three different old- and new-law railroad benefits, supplemental railroad annuities, and an additional Social Security benefit based on pre-1975 non-railroad employment. Benefits are paid directly to the beneficiary in the form of cash, without any restriction on its use, in monthly amounts up to $762 (average $363) for the worker and $312 (average $168) for the dependent spouse, plus up to $70 (average $60) for the supplemental annuity. Some 500,000 persons receive monthly benefits under the program. Benefits are not directly conditioned on need. Benefits are financed by employee and employer contributions, general revenues and transfers from Social Security funds.

A

Authorization: Railroad Retirement Act of 1937, PL74-271 as amended; Railroad Retirement Act of 1974, PL93-445, 45 USC 231-231t.

Budget Code: 60-8011-0-7-601

Catalog Code: 57.001

FY77 Expenditure (est.)

$2,250 million

EXCLUSION OF RAILROAD RETIREMENT BENEFITS

Internal Revenue Service, Department of Treasury

Additional financial assistance is provided indirectly to individuals who receive Railroad Retirement payments during the year. Benefits are in the form of tax relief, funded by allowing the beneficiaries to exclude from consideration as income those basic grant payments received pursuant to the Railroad Retirement Act. (Supplemental annuity payments are taxed as employee pensions.) Benefits are not directly conditioned on need.

B

Authorization: Railroad Retirement Act, as amended, 45 USC 228.

Budget Code: none

Catalog Code: none

FY77 Expenditure (est.)

$200 million

Represents estimated FY77 revenue loss. About 52% of such tax expenditures go to tax filers with adjusted gross incomes under $7,000; and 32%, to those between $7,000 and $15,000.

CIVIL SERVICE RETIREMENT PENSIONS

Civil Service Commission

Federal civil service employees who retire at age 62 with at least five years of service, at age 60 with at least 20 years of service, at age 55 with at least 30 years of service, and under certain other circumstances, are provided monthly cash payments to replace income lost through retirement. There is no provision for dependents of retired workers, and payments vary according to length of service and highest average salary. Benefits are directly paid to the beneficiary in the form of cash, without any restriction on its use, and are financed by an employee contribution of seven percent of salary matched by the government. Some 800,000 persons receive monthly benefits under the program. Benefits are not directly conditioned on need.

B

Authorization: 5 USC 8331-8348

Budget Code: 24-0200-0-1-805, 24-8135-0-7-602

Catalog Code: none

FY77 Expenditure (est.)

$6,370 million

MILITARY NONDISABILITY RETIREMENT

Department of Defense;
Coast Guard, Department of Transportation

Regular and Reserve commissioned officers, enlisted members with 20 to 30 years active service, and certain reserve members are provided monthly cash payments to replace income lost through retirement. Payment amounts vary generally according to length of active service and pay grade at retirement. Benefits are in the form of cash, without restrictions on its use, directly paid to the beneficiary in amounts from 50 to 75 percent of basic pay at retirement. Benefits are paid through direct appropriation by Congress each year; there are no contributions from service member's military compensation financing this program. (As contributing participants, members are also eligible for Social Security benefits.) Close to one million persons receive payments monthly. Benefits are not conditioned on need.

B

Authorization: Officer Personnel Act of 1947; Army and Air Force Vitalization and Retirement Equalization Act of 1948; Career Compensation Act of 1949; PL85-422; PL88-132.

Budget Code: 97-0030-0-1-051, 69-0241-0-1-406

Catalog Code: none

FY77 Expenditure (est.)

$7,233 million

SENIOR COMMUNITY SERVICE EMPLOYMENT

Employment and Training Administration, Department of Labor

Low-income persons who are 55 years old and over and who have poor employment prospects are provided part-time work opportunities in community service activities, such as in schools, hospitals, day care centers, parks, etc. Benefits are in the form of cash compensation, funded by 90-percent formula grants to the states, allocated among public and nonprofit private agencies. About 15,000 jobs are provided annually. Benefits are conditioned on need. This program, while compensating individuals for work, is a public employment program.

B

Authorization: Title IX of the Older Americans Act.

Budget Code: 16-0175-0-1-504

Catalog Code: 17.235

FY77 Expenditure (est.)

$74 million

Includes 15% for project administration.

SENIOR OPPORTUNITIES AND SERVICES

Community Services Administration

Low-income persons over 55 years of age are provided with services, as well as employment and volunteer opportunities, under a plan approved by the local community action (anti-poverty) agency, with the aim of facilitating the greater use of, and participation in public services by the elderly poor. Services vary from information and referral to recreational centers to employment or voluntary participation in program projects. Benefits are in kind and in cash compensation, funded by grants which require 30 to 40 percent in local matching. Almost a million elderly are served annually. Benefits are conditioned, in part, on need.

B

Authorization: Economic Opportunity Act of 1964, as amended by the Community Services Act of 1974, Section 222A(7) of PL93-644, 42 USC 2809.

Budget Code: 81-0500-0-1-999

Catalog Code: 49.010

FY77 Expenditure (est.)

$11 million

I. Replacing Lost Earnings

FOSTER GRANDPARENT PROGRAM

ACTION

Low-income persons, age 60 and over, are provided part-time volunteer opportunities relating to the needs of children in residential and nonresidential facilities, including day care and preschool centers, and, more recently, in their own homes. The foster grandparents receive hot meals, stipends of $32 per week for up to 20 hours weekly, and other related services; the children receive supportive personal attention. Thus, benefits are in cash and in kind, funded by 90-percent grants to public and nonprofit private agencies. Approximately 15,000 foster grandparents serve about 45,000 children yearly. Benefits are conditioned, in part, on need.

B

Authorization: Title II, Part B of the Domestic Volunteer Service Act of 1973, PL93-113.

Budget Code: 44-0103-0-1-451

Catalog Code: 72.001

FY77 Expenditure (est.)

$40 million

Includes over 20% for administration and other support.

SENIOR COMPANION PROGRAM

ACTION

Low-income persons, age 60 and over, are provided part-time volunteer opportunities relating to the needs of adults in residential and nonresidential facilities, and, more recently, in their own homes. The senior companions receive hot meals, stipends of $32 per week for up to 20 hours weekly, and other related services; the adults receive supportive personal attention. Thus, benefits are in cash and in kind, funded by 90-percent grants to public and nonprofit private agencies. Approximately 3,000 senior companions serve as many as 12,000 adults yearly. Benefits are conditioned, in part, on need.

B

Authorization: Title II, Part B of the Domestic Volunteer Service Act of 1973, PL93-113, as amended.

Budget Code: 44-0103-0-1-451

Catalog Code: 72.008

FY77 Expenditure (est.)

$9 million

Includes over 20% for administration and other support.

SOCIAL SECURITY — DISABILITY INSURANCE

Social Security Administration, Department of Health, Education & Welfare

Physically and mentally disabled persons and their dependents are provided monthly cash payments, if the disabled person has worked for a sufficient period of time to be insured. Benefits may not be granted for the first five months of disability. Thereafter, payments are made throughout the period of disability to replace income lost through loss of work. Benefits are directly paid to the beneficiary in the form of cash, without any restrictions on its use, in a monthly amount that ranges from $108 minimum for a disabled individual to $992 maximum for a family. On the average, more than 2.5 million disabled persons and two million of their dependents receive such benefits monthly. As social insurance, benefits are not directly conditioned on need as much as on past contributions by which the program is financed.

A

Authorization: Social Security Act, as amended by PL92-603, PL93-66, and PL93-233, 42 USC 420-425.

Budget Code: 20-8007-0-7-601

Catalog Code: 13.802

FY77 Expenditure (est.)

$11,625 million

RAILROAD DISABILITY INSURANCE

Railroad Retirement Board

Physically and mentally disabled workers with 10 years or more railroad employment are provided monthly cash payments, as are workers with 20 years or more service, disabled only for their regular railroad occupation. The payments are made throughout the period of disability to replace income lost through loss of work; and they may consist of from two to six components: Social Security benefits; three different old- and new-law railroad benefits; supplemental railroad annuities; and an additional Social Security benefit based on pre-1975 non-railroad employment. Benefits are directly paid to the beneficiary in the form of cash, without any restriction on its use, in monthly amounts up to $762 (average $332) plus $70 (average $60) for the supplemental annuity. Over 100,000 persons receive monthly benefits under the program. Benefits are not directly conditioned on need. Benefits are financed by employee and employer contributions, general revenues, and transfers from Social Security funds.

A

Authorization: Railroad Retirement Act of 1937, PL74-271 as amended; Railroad Retirement Act of 1974, PL93-445, 45 USC 231-231t.

Budget Code: 60-8011-0-7-601

Catalog Code: 57.001

FY77 Expenditure (est.)

$551 million

VETERANS COMPENSATION FOR SERVICE-CONNECTED DISABILITIES

Department of Veterans Benefits, Veterans Administration

Non-dishonorably discharged veterans with service-connected disabilities, as well as the dependents of such veterans who are at least 50-percent disabled, are provided monthly payments which vary according to the severity of the disability. Benefits are in the form of cash, funded by direct monthly Federal payments without restrictions on their use, ranging from $38 for a 10-percent disability to over $1,700 for loss of limbs or for blindness. Almost 2,250,000 disabled veterans receive compensation annually, for themselves and their 610,000 dependents, with an average yearly payment of just over $2,000. Benefits are not directly conditioned on need.

A

Authorization: 38 USC 310, 311, as amended by PL94-169, PL94-432 and PL94-433.

Budget Code: 36-0102-0-1-701

Catalog Code: 64.109

FY77 Expenditure (est.)

$4,796 million

VETERANS PENSIONS FOR NON-SERVICE-CONNECTED DISABILITIES

Department of Veterans Benefits, Veterans Administration

Non-dishonorably discharged veterans with active wartime service whose disabilities are considered permanent and total but are not necessarily due to service, and whose income and assets are below certain levels, are provided monthly payments for themselves and their dependants. Veterans, age 65 or older, who meet the wartime service criteria are deemed to be permanently and totally disabled. Benefits are in the form of cash, funded by direct Federal payments without restrictions on their use. Monthly rates vary from a minimum of $5 for a single veteran to $209 for a veteran with three dependents. Additional allowances are provided to veterans who are housebound or in need of aid and attendance. Approximately 1,040,000 veterans receive pensions annually, for themselves and their 840,000 dependents, with an average yearly payment of close to $1,800 per case. Benefits are conditioned on need.

A

Authorization: 38 USC, 510-512, 521, as amended by PL94-169 and PL94-432.

Budget Code: 36-0102-0-1-701

Catalog Code: 64.104

FY77 Expenditure (est.)

$1,870 million

40

EXCLUSION OF VETERANS PENSIONS AND DISABILITY COMPENSATION

Internal Revenue Service, Department of Treasury

Additional financial assistance is provided indirectly to individuals who receive veterans service-connected disability compensation or non-service-connected pensions. Benefits are in the form of tax relief, funded by allowing the veterans (or their survivors) to exclude such payments from consideration as income. (In fact, all benefits and services of the Veterans Administration are non-taxable.) Over 90 percent of this tax relief goes to compensation recipients who tend to have higher incomes and therefore higher marginal tax rates than pension cases. Benefits are not directly conditioned on need.

B

Authorization: 38 USC 3101.

Budget Code: none

Catalog Code: none

FY77 Expenditure (est.)

$685 million

Represents estimated FY77 revenue loss. About 33% of such tax expenditures go to tax filers with adjusted gross incomes under $7,000; and 34%, to those between $7,000 and $15,000.

CIVIL SERVICE DISABILITY PENSIONS

Civil Service Commission

Physically and mentally disabled Federal civil service employees with five or more years of service are provided monthly cash payments throughout the period of disability to replace the income lost through loss of work. There is no provision for dependents of disabled workers, and payments vary according to length of service and highest average salary. Income and earnings from non-civil service employment do not affect the pension as long as such earnings do not exceed 80 percent of the last civil service salary for each of two consecutive years. Benefits are directly paid to the beneficiary in the form of cash, without any restriction on its use, and are financed by an employee contribution of seven percent of salary matched by the government. Almost 300,000 persons receive monthly benefits under the program. Benefits are not directly conditioned on need.

B

Authorization: 5 USC 8331-8348

Budget Code: 24-0200-0-1-805, 24-8135-0-7-602

Catalog Code: none

FY77 Expenditure (est.)

$1,694 million

DISABLED COAL MINE WORKERS BENEFITS AND COMPENSATION

Social Security Administration, Department of Health, Education & Welfare and Employment Standards Administration, Department of Labor

Coal miners disabled by black lung disease and their dependents, as well as the widows of such miners and the dependent surviving children, parents or siblings, are provided monthly payments to replace income lost through disability or death. Benefits are directly paid to the beneficiary in the form of cash, without any restrictions on its use. Benefits on pre-1973 claims are funded by appropriations from general revenues to the Social Security Administration, and they represent 95 percent of program expenditures. New claims are the responsibility of the Department of Labor, and liability is shared with coal mine operators and their insurers. The basic benefit is $205 monthly for a single person, with increments for dependents, subject to other income in some specified circumstances. About 480,000 beneficiaries are aided annually. Benefits are not directly conditioned on need.

A

Authorization: Federal Coal Mine Health and Safety Act of 1969, PL91-173, as amended by PL92-303.

Budget Code: 75-0409-0-1-601, 16-1521-0-1-600

Catalog Code: 13.806, 17.307

FY77 Expenditure (est.)

$935 million

EXCLUSION OF SPECIAL BENEFITS FOR DISABLED COAL MINERS

Internal Revenue Service, Department of Treasury

Additional financial assistance is provided indirectly to individuals receiving disability and survivor payments for coal miners during the year. Benefits are in the form of tax relief, funded by allowing the coal miners or their survivors to exclude from consideration as income the payments so received. Benefits are not directly conditioned on need.

B

Authorization: Revenue rulings under Section 61 of the Internal Revenue Code of 1954, as amended.

Budget Code: none

Catalog Code: none

FY77 Expenditure (est.)

$50 million

Represents estimated FY77 revenue loss. About 52% of such tax expenditures go to tax filers with adjusted gross incomes under $7,000; and 32%, to those between $7,000 and $15,000.

MILITARY DISABILITY RETIREMENT

Department of Defense;
Coast Guard, Department of Transportation

Members of the armed forces with 20 years of service or a 30-percent or more service-connected permanent disability rating are provided monthly cash payments if physically unfit to perform the duties of their pay grade. If disability is not permanent, payments may be made for up to five years, before which time the member must be returned to active duty or reclassified to permanent disability. Payment amounts vary generally according to the percentage of disability, length of service and grade. Benefits are in the form of cash, without restrictions on its use, paid directly to the beneficiary in amounts from 30 to 75 percent of last basic pay. Benefits are paid through direct appropriation by Congress each year; there are no contributions from service member's military compensation financing this program. (As contributing participants, members are also eligible for Social Security benefits.) Over 140,000 persons receive permanent disability benefits; and 12,000, temporary benefits. Benefits are not directly conditioned on need.

B

Authorization: Officer Personnel Act of 1947; Army and Air Force Vitalization and Retirement Equalization Act of 1948; Career Compensation Act of 1949; PL85-422; PL88-132.

Budget Code: 97-0030-0-1-051, 69-0241-0-1-406

Catalog Code: none

FY77 Expenditure (est.)

$980 million

EXCLUSION OF MILITARY DISABILITY PENSIONS

Internal Revenue Service, Department of Treasury

Additional financial assistance is provided indirectly to individuals collecting military disability retirement pay. Benefits are in the form of tax relief, funded by allowing the retired members to exclude from consideration as income the benefits received for military disability. For benefits based solely on percentage of disability, the full amount is excluded from gross income; for benefits based on years of service, only the portion that would have been paid on a disability basis is excluded. Benefits are not directly conditioned on need.

B

Authorization: Section 104(a) (4) of the Internal Revenue Code of 1954, as amended, and Section 1.104-1(e) of the Income Tax Regulations.

Budget Code: none

Catalog Code: none

FY77 Expenditure (est.)

$105 million

Represents estimated FY77 revenue loss. About 46% of such tax expenditures go to tax filers with adjusted gross incomes under $7,000; and 37%, to those between $7,000 and $15,000.

LONGSHOREMEN'S AND HARBOR WORKERS' COMPENSATION

Employment Standards Administration, Department of Labor

Longshoremen, harbor workers, certain other private employees engaged in maritime employment, and employees of private concerns of the District of Columbia and their survivors are provided monthly payments to replace income lost through disability or death. Vocational rehabilitation and certain medical, surgical and related services may also be paid for. Benefits are in the form of cash, with no restrictions on use, paid directly to the beneficiary and funded by appropriations from general revenues, from the Special Workers' Compensation Trust Fund, and from insured employers. Fourteen thousand beneficiaries receive monthly payments. Benefits are not directly conditioned on need.

B

Authorization: Longshoremen's and Harbor Workers' Compensation Act, as amended and extended, 33 USC 901-952, 42 USC 1651, 43 USC 1331, 5 USC 1871, PL92-576.

Budget Code: 16-1521-0-1-600, 16-9971-0-7-601

Catalog Code: 17.302

FY77 Expenditure (est.)

$6 million

FEDERAL EMPLOYEES COMPENSATION BENEFITS

Employment Standards Administration, Department of Labor

Federal employees who are suffering job-related injuries or diseases are provided coverage for associated medical and rehabilitation costs as well as for lost earnings. For total disability, benefits are paid based on two thirds of the employee's monthly pay, or on three fourths, if there are dependents. Death benefits are paid to survivors in amounts ranging from 50 to 75 percent of the deceased's monthly pay. Benefits are in the form of cash, without restrictions on its use, paid directly to the beneficiary. About 45,000 long-term cases receive monthly benefits, and an equal number of new claims are received annually. Benefits are not directly conditioned on need.

B

Authorization: Federal Employees Compensation Act of 1916, as amended.

Budget Code: 16-1521-0-1-600

Catalog Code: none

FY77 Expenditure (est.)

$589 million

EXCLUSION OF WORKER'S COMPENSATION BENEFITS

Internal Revenue Service, Department of Treasury

Additional financial assistance is provided indirectly to employees who receive worker's compensation payments. Benefits are in the form of tax relief, funded by allowing the employee to exclude from consideration as income the payments so received. The exclusion applies both to payments during periods of illness and to those for permanent injuries. These amounts are specified by state laws. Benefits are not directly conditioned on need.

B

Authorization: Section 104(a)(1) of the Internal Revenue Code of 1954, as amended.

Budget Code: none

Catalog Code: none

FY77 Expenditure (est.)

$705 million

Represents estimated FY77 revenue loss. About 22% of such tax expenditures go to tax filers with adjusted gross incomes under $7,000; and 39%, to those between $7,000 and $15,000.

EXCLUSION OF SICK PAY FOR THE DISABLED

Internal Revenue Service, Department of Treasury

Additional financial assistance is provided indirectly to the permanently and totally disabled, under age 65, who receive disability payments from job-related accident or health plans. Benefits are in the form of tax relief, funded by allowing the beneficiaries to exclude from consideration as income the support so received, up to certain limits. The exclusion is reduced, dollar for dollar, for adjusted gross income (including disability payments) in excess of $15,000 yearly. Benefits are conditioned, in part, on need.

B

Authorization: Section 105 (d) of the Internal Revenue Code of 1954, as amended by the Tax Reform Act of 1976.

Budget Code: none

Catalog Code: none

FY77 Expenditure (est.)

$50 million

Represents estimated FY77 revenue loss. Under former provisions, about 17% of such tax expenditures went to tax filers with adjusted gross incomes under $7,000; and 35%, to those between $7,000 and $15,000.

HANDICAPPED ASSISTANCE LOANS

Small Business Administration

Handicapped individuals who cannot engage in normal competitive business practices are provided 15-year loans of up to $350,000 to construct, expand or convert facilities; to purchase buildings, equipment and materials; and for working capital. Nonprofit sheltered workshops for the handicapped are provided similar loans to enable them to produce marketable goods and services, but not for training, housing or other supportive services. Benefits are in the form of favorable credit terms, funded by direct, immediate participation or guaranteed loans. Benefits are not directly conditioned on need.

C

Authorization: Small Business Act, PL85-536, as amended by Section 3 of the PL93-595, 15 USC 686.

Budget Code: 73-4154-0-3-403

Catalog Code: 59.021

FY77 Expenditure (est.)

$13 million

Loan fund capital outlays and operating expenses in FY77 are partially offset by receipts, including repayments, recoveries and interest revenue. Estimated FY77 loan commitments are $14 million.

SOCIAL SECURITY—
SURVIVORS INSURANCE

Social Security Administration, Department of Health, Education & Welfare

Dependents of deceased workers are provided monthly cash payments, if the deceased worker had worked for a sufficient period of time to be insured; and the payments are made to replace income lost through his or her death. Benefits are directly paid to the beneficiary in the form of cash, without any restrictions on its use, in a monthly amount that ranges from $108 minimum for a sole survivor to $992 maximum for a family. On the average, 7.5 million survivors receive such benefits monthly. As social insurance, benefits are not directly conditioned on need as much as on past contributions by which the program is financed.

A

Authorization: Social Security Act, as amended by PL92-603, PL93-66, and PL93-233, 42 USC 401-429.

Budget Code: 20-8006-0-7-601

Catalog Code: 13.805

FY77 Expenditure (est.)

$18,888 million

RAILROAD SURVIVORS INSURANCE

Railroad Retirement Board

Widows, widowers, dependent children, and certain dependent parents of deceased railroad workers with 10 years or more of railroad employment are provided monthly cash payments to replace the lost earnings of the deceased. Such payments are similar to Social Security survivors benefits, but consist of from two to four components. Benefits are directly paid to the beneficiary in the form of cash, without any restriction on its use, in monthly amounts up to $573 (average $257). Some 400,000 persons receive monthly benefits under the program. Benefits are not directly conditioned on need. Benefits are financed by employee and employer contributions, general revenues and transfers from Social Security funds.

A

Authorization: Railroad Retirement Act of 1937, PL74-271 as amended; Railroad Retirement Act of 1974, PL93-445, 43 USC 231-231t.

Budget Code: 60-8011-0-7-601

Catalog Code: 57.001

FY77 Expenditure (est.)

$1,026 million

SURVIVORS COMPENSATION FOR SERVICE-CONNECTED DEATHS

Department of Veterans Benefits, Veterans Administration

Surviving widows, widowers, children and certain parents of non-dishonorably discharged veterans who died because of a service-connected disability are provided monthly payments which vary by family size, special needs, and the military pay grade and year of death of the veteran. Parents must meet certain income criteria for eligibility. Benefits are in the form of cash, funded by direct Federal payments without restrictions on their use. Almost 90,000 dependent parents receive benefits, averaging $900 yearly, for veterans who died before January, 1957. Benefits are provided to about 65,000 other parents, 210,000 unmarried widows and widowers, and 110,000 children of those veterans who have died subsequent to January, 1957. Payments per case average almost $3,000 annually. Only for surviving parents are benefits directly conditioned on need. The pre-1957 program is distinct from the post-1957 one in rules and benefit levels. However, only 10 per cent of expenditures are for pre-1957 coverage.

A

Authorization: 38 USC 321, 341, 410, 411, 413, 415 as amended by PL94-169, PL94-432 and PL94-433.

Budget Code: 36-0102-0-1-701

Catalog Code: 64.102, 64.110

FY77 Expenditure (est.)

$1,067 million

VETERANS SURVIVORS PENSIONS

Department of Veterans Benefits, Veterans Administration

Unmarried widows and widowers and dependent children of deceased, non-dishonorably discharged, wartime veterans' whose deaths were not due to service are provided monthly payments if their incomes and assets are below certain levels. Benefits are in the form of cash, funded by direct Federal payments without restrictions on their use. Monthly rates vary from a minimum of $5 for a single widow or widower to $149 for a widow or widower with one child, and $24 for each additional child, as well as an additional $74 if aid or attendance is required. Approximately 910,000 widows and widowers and 700,000 children receive pensions annually, with an average yearly payment of just over $1,000 per case. Benefits are conditioned on need.

A

Authorization: 38 USC 541 and 542, as amended by PL94-169 and PL94-432.

Budget Code: 36-0102-0-1-701

Catalog Code: 64.105

FY77 Expenditure (est.)

$1,322 million

AID TO FAMILIES WITH DEPENDENT CHILDREN

Social and Rehabilitation Service, Department of Health, Education & Welfare

Public assistance to cover the minimum costs of food, shelter, clothing and other items of daily living, is provided on behalf of needy dependent children, generally in broken homes. Such children must be deprived of the support of at least one parent by reason of death, desertion or incapacity. Benefits are directly paid to the children's parents or caretaker relatives in the form of cash, usually without restrictions on its use. Payments are monthly or semi-monthly, in amounts varying according to each family's countable income and needs, as determined under state law. Benefits are funded by formula grants to state welfare agencies. Each state contributes from 17 to 50 percent of assistance costs, depending on its relative per capita income, as well as 50 percent of administrative costs. Each month, on the average, over 10 million recipients in over three million families are aided. Benefits are conditioned on need.

A

Authorization: Title IV of the Social Security Act, as amended, 42 USC 602 *et seq.*, 1301 *et seq.*

Budget Code: 75-0581-0-1-999

Catalog Code: 13.761

FY77 Expenditure (est.)

$5,718 million

Includes over 10% for state and local administration and other support.

BURIAL ALLOWANCE FOR VETERANS

Department of Veterans Benefits, Veterans Administration

Persons who bear the funeral and burial expenses of certain non-dishonorably discharged veterans who die as a result of service-connected disabilities are provided up to $800 to defray the costs. For those who die of other causes, up to $250 is provided, and, if the veteran is not buried in a national cemetery, another $150 is provided toward plot or interment expenses. In all the above cases, an inscribed headstone or marker may be provided for the grave, and transportation costs of the deceased will be paid where death occurs in a VA facility. Approximately 650,000 burial allowances are made annually. Benefits are not conditioned on need.

C

Authorization: 38 USC 901-903, 907, 908 as amended by PL94-433.

Budget Code: 36-0102-0-1-701

Catalog Code: 64.101, 64.202

FY77 Expenditure (est.)

$150 million

CIVIL SERVICE SURVIVORS PENSIONS

Civil Service Commission

Dependent children and certain spouses of deceased retired, Federal civil service employees, as well as unmarried widows and widowers and dependent children of deceased nonretired employees with at least 18 months of service, are provided monthly cash payments to replace the lost pension income of earnings of the deceased. Generally, a spouse's benefit is 55 percent of the retired employee's pension or, in the case of a nonretired worker, the pension the worker had earned at the time of death (with a guaranteed minimum). Child survivors usually receive a flat monthly amount regardless of parent's salary or tenure. Benefits are directly paid to the beneficiary in the form of cash, without any restriction on its use, and are financed by an employee contribution of seven percent of salary matched by the government. Over 400,000 persons receive monthly benefits under the program. Benefits are not directly conditioned on need.

B

Authorization: 5 USC 8331-8348

Budget Code: 24-0200-0-1-805, 24-8135-0-7-602

Catalog Code: none

FY77 Expenditure (est.)

$1,205 million

MILITARY SURVIVORS BENEFITS

Department of Defense;
Coast Guard, Department of Transportation

Surviving unmarried spouses and dependent children of deceased retired military personnel are provided monthly payments to replace benefit income lost through the death of the retiree. Payment amounts vary according to pay grade and certain elected factors. Benefits are in the form of cash, without restrictions on its use, directly paid to the beneficiary. Benefits are reduced by the amount of Social Security Survivors benefits attributable to military service. Over 40,000 persons receive military survivors benefits, which are financed in part by contributions from retirees' annuities. There are two different programs (pre- and post-1972) that make up this benefit: Retired Serviceman's Family Protection Plan (RSFPP) and Survivor Benefit Plan (SBP). While their rules differ, they are both geared to the same objective. Benefits are partly conditioned on need.

B

Authorization: Uniform Services Contingency Option Act of 1953; Servicemen's and Veteran's Survivors' Benefit Act of 1956; PL92-245.

Budget Code: 97-0030-0-1-051, 69-0241-0-1-406

Catalog Code: none

FY77 Expenditure (est.)

$120 million

MEDICAL ASSISTANCE (MEDICAID)

Social and Rehabilitation Service, Department of Health, Education & Welfare

Public assistance recipients and other low-income persons are provided inpatient and outpatient hospital services, laboratory and x-ray services, nursing home services, home health services for persons age 21 and over, early periodic screening and diagnosis and treatment for persons under age 21, family planning services and physicians services. AFDC recipients are automatically eligible in all states. SSI recipients in 35 states are automatically eligible, while in 15 states they must satisfy additional criteria. Medically needy persons (those with equivalent or somewhat higher incomes than, but characteristics similar to, AFDC and SSI recipients) are eligible in over half the states. Benefits are in kind, funded by formula grants to state welfare agencies for the direct purchase of approved services. Each state contributes from 17 to 50 percent of assistance costs, depending on its relative per capita income, as well as 50 percent of administrative costs. Over 24 million persons receive medical care annually. Benefits are conditioned on need.

A

Authorization: Title XIX of the Social Security Act, as amended; PL89-97; PL90-248; PL91-56; PL92-223; PL92-603; PL93-223; 42 USC 1396 *et seq.*

Budget Code: 75-0581-0-1-999

Catalog Code: 13.714

FY77 Expenditure (est.)

$9,859 million

Includes 5% for state and local administration and other support.

I. Replacing Lost Earnings

SOCIAL SERVICES

Social and Rehabilitation Service, Department of Health, Education & Welfare

Public assistance recipients and other low-income persons are provided social services to assist them to be economically self-supporting, to protect children and adults from abuse or neglect, to help families stay together, to prevent inappropriate institutionalization by providing alternate forms of care, and to arrange for appropriate institutionalization. Benefits are in kind, funded by 75-percent formula grants to state welfare agencies for allocation among local districts. Typical services are day care, foster or protective care, homemaking, family planning, and those related to health, mental retardation and drug or alcohol abuse. Day care accounts for approximately one third of expenditures; foster and protective care, for one sixth. Benefits are conditioned on need.

B

Authorization: Title XX, Part A of the Social Security Act Social Services Amendments of 1974, PL93-647, PL94-401, 42 USC 1397 *et seq.*

Budget Code: 75-0581-0-1-999

Catalog Code: 13.754, 13.771

FY77 Expenditure (est.)

$2,645 million

STATE AND COMMUNITY PLANNING AND SERVICES FOR THE AGING

Office of Human Development, Department of Health, Education & Welfare

Older persons, age 60 and over, especially the low-income and minority elderly, are provided a coordinated and comprehensive system of social services to support their self-care in the community. Benefits are in kind, funded by 75-percent and 90-percent formula grants to state agencies on aging for planning, coordination and delivery of services pursuant to area plans. The emphasis is on coordination of existing services and inauguration of needed new services in the community. About 500 area plans have been established. Benefits are not directly conditioned on need.

B

Authorization: Title III of the Older Americans Act of 1965, PL89-73, as amended by PL90-42, PL91-69, PL92-258, PL93-29, PL93-351, and PL94-135, 42 USC 3021-3025.

Budget Code: 75-1636-0-1-500

Catalog Code: 13.633

FY77 Expenditure (est.)

$140 million

MEDICARE — SUPPLEMENTARY MEDICAL INSURANCE

Social Security Administration, Department of Health, Education & Welfare

Except for specified deductibles and coinsurance, the reasonable costs of physicians services, outpatient and related care, are paid directly to participating providers on behalf of nearly all persons who are age 65 and over, as well as disabled persons under age 65 who have been entitled to Social Security or Railroad Retirement benefits for at least two years or who have chronic kidney disease requiring dialysis or transplant. Enrollees pay a monthly premium of $7.70, but some states have elected to pay the premium on behalf of certain qualifying individuals. The other half of the program's cost is met by general revenue appropriations. Benefits are in kind, and approximately 15 million persons receive them annually. Benefits are not directly conditioned on need.

A

Authorization: Title XVIII, Part B of the Social Security Act, as amended in 1965 by PL89-97, and by PL90-248, PL92-603, PL93-233, and PL94-182, 42 USC 1395 *et seq.*

Budget Code: 75-0404-0-1-999, 20-8004-0-7-551

Catalog Code: 13.801

FY77 Expenditure (est.)

$6,330 million

MEDICARE — HOSPITAL INSURANCE

Social Security Administration
Department of Health, Education & Welfare

Except for specified deductibles and coinsurance, the reasonable costs of hospital and related care are paid directly to participating hospitals, skilled nursing facilities and certain other providers on behalf of persons who reached age 65 before 1968, disabled persons under age 65 who have been entitled to Social Security or Railroad Retirement benefits for at least two years or who have chronic kidney disease requiring dialysis or transplant, as well as persons who reached age 65 in 1968 or after with some but not sufficient work credit to qualify for Social Security or Railroad Retirement benefits. The latter group is assisted through general revenue transfers of almost one billion dollars into the Federal Hospital Insurance Trust Fund; the rest are financed by payroll contributions of employers and employees. Benefits are in kind, and approximately six million persons have benefits paid on their behalf annually. Benefits are not directly conditioned on need.

A

Authorization: Title XVIII, Part A of the Social Security Act, as amended in 1965 by PL89-97, and by PL90-248, PL92-603, PL93-233, PL94-182, and PL94-437, 42 USC 1395 *et seq.*

Budget Code: 75-0404-0-1-999, 20-8005-0-7-551

Catalog Code: 13.800

FY77 Expenditure (est.)

$15,314 million

RETIRED FEDERAL EMPLOYEES HEALTH BENEFITS

Civil Service Commission

Beneficiaries of Civil Service retirement, disability and survivors pensions are provided either group health insurance, under the government-sponsored uniform health benefits plan, or contributions to a private health insurance plan. Benefits are in kind, financed by government contributions and withholdings from pensions. Over one million persons elect to be covered by the programs annually. Benefits are not directly conditioned on need.

B

Authorization: Retired Federal Employees Health Benefits Act of 1960, as amended by PL94-310, 5 USC 8331-8348, 8901, 8906.

Budget Code: 24-8440-0-8-551, 24-8445-0-8-551, 24-0206-0-1-805

Catalog Code: none

FY77 Expenditure (est.)

$433 million

Represents Federal contributions on behalf of annuitants into both plans.

NUTRITION PROGRAMS FOR THE ELDERLY

Office of Human Development, Department of Health, Education & Welfare

Older persons (over age 60), especially the low-income and minority elderly, are provided low-cost nutritious meals and supportive services, including health care, education, counseling and recreation. Benefits are in kind, funded by 90-percent formula grants to state agencies on aging, which then allocate the funds among local projects. The non-Federal share may be in cash or in kind. Local projects must provide a hot meal at least once a day, five days a week, to the elderly and their spouses. More than 400,000 meals, at over 8,000 sites, are served daily by the program. Benefits are not directly conditioned on need.

A

Authorization: Title VII of the Older Americans Act of 1965, PL89-73, as amended by PL90-42, PL91-69, PL92-258, PL93-29, PL93-351, and PL94-135, 42 USC 3001 *et seq.*

Budget Code: 12-3511-0-1-604, 75-1636-0-1-500

Catalog Code: 13.635

FY77 Expenditure (est.)

$209 million

Includes over $20 million in distributed commodities.

EXCLUSION FROM CAPITAL GAIN ON HOME SALES BY THE ELDERLY

Internal Revenue Service, Department of Treasury

Indirect financial assistance is provided, once in their lifetime, to elderly taxpayers who sell their homes but do not buy replacement homes. Benefits are in the form of tax relief, funded by allowing such taxpayers to exclude from consideration as income the capital gain realized on the sale of their residences. The exclusion applies, to taxpayers of age 65 or older, on gains on the first $35,000 of adjusted sales price. This provision is intended to assist those elderly who wish to sell their houses and rent apartments or make other living arrangements, but the benefits are more concentrated among higher income taxpayers. Benefits are not conditioned on need.

C

Authorization: Section 121 of the Internal Revenue Code of 1954, as amended by the Tax Reform Act of 1976.

Budget Code: none

Catalog Code: none

FY77 Expenditure (est.)

$40 million

Represents estimated FY77 revenue loss. Under former provisions, about 10% of such tax expenditures went to tax filers with adjusted gross incomes under $7,000; and 20%, to those between $7,000 and $15,000.

HOUSING FOR THE ELDERLY AND HANDICAPPED

Department of Housing & Urban Development

Rental and cooperative housing and related facilities like central dining are provided for lower-income persons who are elderly, physically handicapped or developmentally disabled. Benefits are in kind to these occupants, funded by direct loans at favorable credit terms to private nonprofit corporations and consumer cooperatives. (The receipts and disbursements of the loan fund are not included in the Federal Budget, by law.) The 40-year loans are in effect 100 percent, since any financing commitments imposed upon the developer are returned when rent-up is completed. This program is to be used in conjunction with Section 8 housing assistance payments. Financing for 25,000 units will be provided this year. Benefits are conditioned on need.

A

Authorization: Section 202 of the Housing Act of 1959, as amended; Section 210(d) of the Housing and Community Development Act of 1974; 12 USC 1701q.

Budget Code: 86-4115-0-3-401

Catalog Code: 14.157

FY77 Expenditure (est.)

$262 million

Most of loan fund capital outlays in FY77 are to be retained as undisbursed loans. Estimated FY77 loan commitments are $1.5 billion.

RENT SUPPLEMENTS

Housing Production and Mortgage Credit, Department of Housing & Urban Development

Low-income families that contain elderly or handicapped persons or that live in substandard or damaged units are provided good quality rental housing at rents equal to at least 25 percent of adjusted income. Benefits are in kind, funded by direct Federal payments to owners of approved multifamily rental housing projects. These payments make up the difference between the tenants' partial rental and the market rent. This program was operated in conjunction with various mortgage insurance subprograms, with the rent supplement contract running for the life of the mortgage, or up to 40 years. About 300,000 units are eligible for rent supplements. New commitments will not be made under this program except when they cannot be accommodated under the Lower Income Housing Assistance (Section 8) program. Benefits are conditioned on need.

A

Authorization: Housing and Urban Development Act of 1965, PL89-117, 12 USC 1701(s).

Budget Code: 86-0129-0-1-604, 86-0139-0-1-604

Catalog Code: 14.149

FY77 Expenditure (est.)

$245 million

VERY LOW-INCOME HOUSING REPAIR LOANS

Farmers Home Administration, Department of Agriculture

Very low-income, rural homeowners (mainly elderly or handicapped) are provided loans at a subsidized one-percent interest rate, for terms of up to 20 years, to make essential repairs to their homes, including those to the foundation, roof, basic structure, and water and waste disposal systems. Benefits are in the form of favorable credit terms on direct loans up to $5,000, funded from the Rural Housing Insurance Fund. Over 6,000 loans are to be made in 1977 to persons whose incomes are so low they cannot qualify for regular home repair loans (*e.g.,* under the Low to Moderate Rural Housing Loan Program). About 2,000 grants are also to be made to persons of age 62 or older who are unable to repay the part of the assistance they receive in loan form. Benefits are conditioned on need.

B

Authorization: Section 504 of the Housing Act of 1949, as amended, 42 USC 1474.

Budget Code: 12-4141-0-3-401, 12-2064-0-1-604

Catalog Code: 10.417

FY77 Expenditure (est.)

$5 million

Loan fund capital outlays and operating expenses in FY77 are to be more than offset by receipts, including sales of beneficial ownership certificates. Estimated FY77 loan commitments are $15 million; grant outlays, $5 million.

SPECIALLY ADAPTED HOUSING FOR DISABLED VETERANS

Department of Veterans Benefits, Veterans Administration

Non-dishonorably discharged veterans with permanent, total and compensable disabilities of loss of use of both lower extremities, or both eyes and one lower extremity, or one lower extremity and other organs are provided financial aid toward ownership of a home adapted for their use. Benefits are in the form of cash, funded by direct payments, restricted for a specific use; and they provide 50 percent of the housing unit's cost up to $25,000. Almost 600 disabled veterans receive housing grants annually. Benefits are not directly conditioned on need.

C

Authorization: PL80-702, PL92-341, 38 USC 801-806.

Budget Code: 36-0137-0-1-702

Catalog Code: 64.106

FY77 Expenditure (est.)

$14 million

VETERANS HOSPITALIZATION

Department of Medicine and Surgery, Veterans Administration

Non-dishonorably discharged veterans with service-connected disabilities or diseases, those without service-connected disabilities unable to pay the cost of necessary hospital care, and those over age 65 or in receipt of a veterans pension are provided inpatient, medical, surgical and psychiatric care, related medical and dental services, and hospital-based home health care following discharge from inpatient status. Benefits are in kind, funded principally by means of the salaries and expenses of personnel assigned to VA hospital facilities. Approximately 1,210,000 veterans are treated as inpatients annually, with an average daily census of 76,000. Benefits are conditioned, in part, on need.

B

Authorization: 38 USC Chapter 17.

Budget Code: 36-0160-0-1-703

Catalog Code: 64.009

FY77 Expenditure (est.)

$2,862 million

VETERANS CONTRACT HOSPITALIZATION

Department of Medicine and Surgery, Veterans Administration

When VA facilities are not available, veterans with service-connected disabilities or diseases and an emergent condition are provided inpatient, medical, surgical and psychiatric care in contract facilities. Such facilities can be either other Federal hospitals or, under specified conditions, non-Federal hospitals. Benefits are in kind, funded by the purchase of services in the contracted hospitals. Approximately 32,000 veterans are treated annually in contract facilities, with an average daily census of 1,350. Benefits are conditioned, in part, on need.

B

Authorization: 38 USC 601, 1506.

Budget Code: 36-0160-0-1-703

Catalog Code: none

FY77 Expenditure (est.)

$55 million

VETERANS OUTPATIENT CARE

Department of Medicine and Surgery, Veterans Administration

Outpatient medical and dental services are provided to veterans with a disease, injury or disability that is service-related, or that is aggravating a service-related condition, to veterans requiring outpatient care to obviate the need for hospitalization, and to certain other veterans including the permanently housebound. Benefits are in kind, funded principally by the salaries and expenses of personnel assigned to VA hospitals, and, under certain conditions, by the purchase of service on a fee basis from hometown physicians and dentists. Outpatient medical visits to VA facilities annually number about 14 million; to hometown physicians, 2 million; dental examinations at VA facilities, 94,000; dental treatments at VA facilities, 95,000; and dental visits to hometown dentists, 120,000. Benefits are not directly conditioned on need.

B

Authorization: 38 USC Chapter 17; 38 USC 612.

Budget Code: 36-0160-0-1-703
Catalog Code: 64.011

FY77 Expenditure (est.)

$872 million

CIVILIAN HEALTH AND MEDICAL PROGRAM—VA

Department of Medicine and Surgery, Veterans Administration

Certain dependents and survivors of non-dishonorably discharged veterans are provided the full range of hospital and outpatient services in private facilities. Those eligible are spouses and children of permanently and totally disabled veterans with service-connected conditions, and the widows, widowers and children of veterans who died as a result of service-connected disabilities. Benefits are in kind, funded by the purchase of services by the VA. The average daily inpatient census is 500, and outpatient visits number over 175,000 annually. Benefits are not directly conditioned on need.

B

Authorization: 38 USC Chapter 17, 38 USC 613.

Budget Code: 36-0160-0-1-703

Catalog Code: none

FY77 Expenditure (est.)

$29 million

VETERANS PRESCRIPTION SERVICE

Department of Medicine and Surgery, Veterans Administration

Non-dishonorably discharged veterans eligible for VA outpatient care, as well as veterans whose pension payments have been discontinued because their increased annual income exceeds the allowable maximum, but by less than $500, are provided prescription drugs and expendable medical supplies from VA pharmacies upon presentation of a prescription from a licensed physician. Transactions may be direct or by mail. Benefits are in kind, funded by the VA purchase of medicines, drugs and medical supplies for distribution. Close to two million prescriptions are filled annually. Benefits are conditioned, in part, on need.

B

Authorization: PL91-500, PL93-82, and PL94-581, 38 USC 612.

Budget Code: 36-0160-0-1-703

Catalog Code: 64.012

FY77 Expenditure (est.)

$12 million

VETERANS PROSTHETIC APPLIANCES

Department of Medicine and Surgery, Veterans Administration

Prosthetic and related appliances and services are provided to, or repaired for, disabled veterans eligible for VA outpatient care; veterans receiving hospital, nursing home, or domiciliary care in VA facilities or at VA expense; and certain other veterans receiving VA compensation or pensions. Benefits are in kind, funded by the purchase of prosthetic appliances, including artificial limbs and eyes, wheelchairs, crutches and canes, hearing aids, braces, orthopedic shoes and eyeglasses. Over 1,500,000 prosthetic devices and repair services are provided annually. Benefits are conditioned, in part, on need.

B

Authorization: PL79-268, 38 USC 601, 610, 612-614, 617, 623, 624, 1506, 1901-13, 5013.

Budget Code: 36-0160-0-1-703

Catalog Code: 64.013

FY77 Expenditure (est.)

$50 million

BLIND VETERANS REHABILITATION CENTERS

Department of Medicine and Surgery, Veterans Administration

Non-dishonorably discharged blind veterans are provided personal and social adjustment assistance, as well as rehabilitation, medical and health-related services, for approximately four months, at one of three centers. Benefits are in kind, funded principally by means of the salaries and expenses of VA personnel assigned to the centers. About 650 blind veterans and servicemen go through the centers annually. Benefits are not directly conditioned on need.

C

Authorization: 38 USC 610, 3021.

Budget Code: 36-0160-0-1-703

Catalog Code: 64.007

FY77 Expenditure (est.)

$3 million

VETERANS NURSING HOME CARE

Department of Medicine and Surgery, Veterans Administration

Non-dishonorably discharged veterans requiring skilled nursing home care and related medical and personal adjustment services for a protracted period of time are provided such care in VA facilities. Benefits are in kind, funded principally by means of the salaries and expenses of personnel assigned to VA nursing homes. Approximately 11,000 veterans are treated annually, with an average census of over 7,000. Benefits are not directly conditioned on need.

B

Authorization: PL88-450, PL89-311, PL89-358, PL91-500, PL93-82 and PL94-581, 38 USC 610 and 5001.

Budget Code: 36-0160-0-1-703

Catalog Code: 64.010

FY77 Expenditure (est.)

$147 million

COMMUNITY NURSING HOME CARE

Department of Medicine and Surgery, Veterans Administration

Non-dishonorably discharged veterans with service-connected conditions requiring skilled nursing home care are provided unlimited care in contracted private facilities when VA facilities are not available. Benefits are in the form of cash payments for a restricted use, authorized monthly. Approximately 28,000 veterans are treated annually, with an average daily census of 8,000. Benefits are not directly conditioned on need.

B

Authorization: PL88-450, PL90-612, PL91-101, PL93-82 and PL94-581, 38 USC 620.

Budget Code: 36-0160-0-1-703

Catalog Code: 64.002

FY77 Expenditure (est.)

$75 million

VETERANS DOMICILIARY CARE

Department of Medicine and Surgery, Veterans Administration

Non-dishonorably discharged veterans with service-connected disabilities and no adequate means of support, veterans suffering from permanent disabilities and in receipt of disability compensation, and certain other such veterans unable to defray the costs of necessary domiciliary care, are provided medical assistance, and physical, social and psychological support in a sheltered environment. Emphasis is placed on motivating those veterans who are capable of returning to the community and to be self-supporting. Benefits are in kind, funded principally by means of the salaries and expenses of the personnel assigned to VA domiciliary care facilities. Approximately 18,000 veterans are treated annually, with an average daily census of 9,000. Benefits are conditioned, in part, on need.

B

Authorization: PL87-583, PL89-358, and PL94-581, 38 USC 610; Executive Order 5398, July 21, 1930.

Budget Code: 36-0160-0-1-703

Catalog Code: 64.008

FY77 Expenditure (est.)

$69 million

VETERANS GRANTS FOR STATE HOME CARE

Department of Medicine and Surgery, Veterans Administration

Domiciliary care, nursing home care and hospital care are provided in state veterans homes to veterans, if they have a service-connected disability, or if they receive or would be eligible for disability compensation, or if they have a non-service-connected disability for which they are unable to defray the expenses of necessary care, and if they are not dishonorably discharged. Benefits are in kind, funded by formula grants to the states offsetting a share of the per diem rate for care in state veterans facility or home. For domiciliary care, the number of veterans treated annually approximates 13,000, with an average daily census of 6,000. The respective figures for nursing home care are 10,000 and 5,000; for hospital care, 7,000 and 1,000. Benefits are conditioned, in part, on need.

B

Authorization: PL88-450, PL93-82, PL94-417 and PL94-581, 38 USC 641-643.

Budget Code: 36-0160-0-1-703

Catalog Code: 64.014, 64.015, 64.016

FY77 Expenditure (est.)

$36 million

DEVELOPMENTAL DISABILITIES — BASIC SUPPORT

Office of Human Development, Department of Health, Education & Welfare

Developmentally disabled persons (*i.e.,* those suffering substantial handicaps resulting from mental retardation, cerebral palsy, epilepsy, or other neurological conditions developed in childhood) are provided care, training, legal and other services. Benefits are in kind, funded mainly by formula grants to designated state agencies. The Federal matching percentage is somewhat higher in poverty areas. About 50,000 individuals receive services annually. Benefits are not directly conditioned on need.

C

Authorization: Mental Retardation Facilities and Community Mental Health Centers Construction Act of 1963, PL88-164, as amended by PL91-517 and by PL94-103, the Developmentally Disabled Assistance and Bill of Rights Act.

Budget Code: 75-1636-0-1-500

Catalog Code: 13.630

FY77 Expenditure (est.)

$32 million

About half these funds are to be used for planning, administration, facilities construction, and other support.

II
PROGRAMS PROVIDING BENEFITS TO SUPPLEMENT THE EARNED INCOME OF THE FAMILY

AID TO FAMILIES WITH DEPENDENT CHILDREN — UNEMPLOYED FATHER

Social and Rehabilitation Service, Department of Health, Education & Welfare

Public assistance to cover the minimum costs of food, shelter, clothing, and other items of daily living is provided on behalf of needy dependent children in intact families. Such a child must be deprived of the support of his or her father by virtue of his unemployment. The father must meet certain requirements regarding past work history and must be at least partially unemployed. Benefits are directly paid to the children's parents in the form of cash, usually without restrictions on its use. Payments are monthly or semi-monthly, in amounts varying according to each family's countable income and needs, as determined under state law. (Only half the states have elected to operate this program.) Benefits are funded by formula grants to state welfare agencies; and each state contributes from 17 to 50 percent of assistance costs, depending on its relative per capita income, as well as 50 percent of administrative costs. Each month, on the average, about 700,000 recipients in 150,000 families are aided. Benefits are conditioned on need.

A

Authorization: Title IV of the Social Security Act, as amended, 42 USC 602 *et seq.*, 1301 *et seq.*

Budget Code: 75-0581-0-1-999

Catalog Code: 13.761

FY77 Expenditure (est.)

$400 million

Includes over 10% for state and local administration and other support.

FEDERAL–STATE UNEMPLOYMENT INSURANCE

Employment and Training Administration, Department of Labor

Workers in covered employment who are involuntarily unemployed, but able to and available for work, and who have accumulated enough work credits (based on time and wages) are provided weekly payments to replace their lost earnings. Benefits are paid directly to the individual in the form of cash, without restrictions on its use, funded through the states from the Unemployment Trust Fund, which is financed by Federal and state taxes on employers' payrolls and by Federal appropriations. Benefits are based on average past weekly earnings and may be reduced by any earnings during the overall period of unemployment, in accordance with state law. Benefits may be extended by two 13-week periods beyond the normal 26-week period, in times of higher unemployment. The Federal government reimburses states for part of the costs of such extended and supplementary benefits. Benefits are not directly conditioned on need. About ten million beneficiaries will be aided this year, and over one third of them will require extended benefits.

A

Authorization: Social Security Act, as amended, 42 USC 501-503, 1101-1105; PL93-567, PL93-572 and PL94-45.

Budget Code: 16-0327-0-1-603, 20-8042-0-7-999, 16-0179-0-1-504

Catalog Code: 17.225

FY77 Expenditure (est.)

$13,490 million

Includes 6% for state administration and other support. A quarter of the outlays are to be for extended and supplementary benefits.

RAILROAD UNEMPLOYMENT INSURANCE

Railroad Retirement Board

Railroad workers in covered employment who are involuntarily unemployed, but able to and available for work, or who are unable to work because of an illness or injury for which no other compensation or remuneration is available are provided biweekly payments if they meet certain earnings and work criteria. Benefit rates are based on claimants' past earnings histories; the maximum weekly rate is $125, and the average is $123. Benefits are in the form of cash without restrictions on its use, funded by direct payments from the railroad account in the unemployment trust fund—which itself is maintained by a tax on employer payrolls. The program's average caseload is 20,000 persons. Benefits are not directly conditioned on need, although earnings from employment, sick pay, and Social Security benefits are considered in determining whether an individual is eligible for aid.

A

Authorization: Railroad Unemployment Insurance Act of 1938, PL75-722, as amended, 45 USC 351-367.

Budget Code: 20-8042-0-7-999

Catalog Code: 57.001

FY77 Expenditure (est.)

$183 million

UNEMPLOYMENT COMPENSATION FOR FEDERAL CIVILIAN EMPLOYEES AND EX-SERVICEMEN

Employment and Training Administration, Department of Labor

Federal civilian workers, postal workers and non-dishonorably discharged ex-servicemen who are involuntarily unemployed, but able to and available for work, are provided benefits to replace their lost earnings. Benefits are paid directly to the individual in the form of cash, without restrictions on its use, funded through the states by Federal appropriations from general revenues covering the full cost of the programs. Benefits are based on the individual's past pay grade and may be reduced by any earnings during the overall period of unemployment, in accordance with state law. Benefits are not directly conditioned on need. Well over a half million beneficiaries will be aided this year; less than one fifth will be ex-servicemen.

A

Authorization: Social Security Act, as amended; 5 USC 8501-8525.

Budget Code: 16-0179-0-1-504, 16-0326-0-1-603

Catalog Code: 17.225

FY77 Expenditure (est.)

$712 million

Includes 6% for state administration and other support.

EXCLUSION OF UNEMPLOYMENT INSURANCE BENEFITS

Internal Revenue Service, Department of Treasury

Additional financial assistance is provided indirectly to individuals who receive unemployment compensation payments during the year. Benefits are in the form of tax relief, funded by allowing the beneficiaries to exclude from consideration as income those payments received as unemployment compensation. Benefits are not directly conditioned on need.

B

Authorization: IRS administrative ruling I.T. 3230 (1938).

Budget Code: none

Catalog Code: none

FY77 Expenditure (est.)

$2,745 million

Represents estimated FY77 revenue loss. About 22% of such tax expenditures go to tax filers with adjusted gross incomes under $7,000; and 39%, to those between $7,000 and $15,000.

EXCLUSION OF EMPLOYER CONTRIBUTIONS TO SUPPLEMENTARY UNEMPLOYMENT INSURANCE TRUSTS

Internal Revenue Service, Department of Treasury

Indirect financial assistance is provided to employed taxpayers to help pay for the cost of maintaining private supplementary unemployment insurance trust funds on their behalf. Benefits are in the form of tax relief, funded by allowing employees to exclude from consideration as income the contributions on their behalf, by their employers, into qualified trusts. The earnings of such trust funds are also non-taxable as they accrue. Thus, employers (generally in industries affected by cyclical and seasonal unemployment) can provide extra unemployment assistance at less cost than if they had to pay taxable wages sufficient for their employees' purchase of such coverage. Benefits are not directly conditioned on need.

B

Authorization: Section 501(c)17 of the Internal Revenue Code of 1954, as amended.

Budget Code: none

Catalog Code: none

FY77 Expenditure (est.)

$10 million

Represents estimated FY77 revenue loss. About 20% of such tax expenditures go to tax filers with adjusted gross incomes under $7,000; and 60%, to those between $7,000 and $15,000.

SPECIAL UNEMPLOYMENT ASSISTANCE

Employment and Training Administration, Department of Labor

Involuntarily unemployed workers, who would be eligible for Federal-state unemployment insurance except for the fact that their occupation or employer is not covered, are provided benefits to replace their lost earnings. Benefits are paid directly to the individual in the form of cash, without restrictions on its use, funded through the states by Federal appropriations from general revenues covering the full cost of the program. Benefits are based on average past weekly earnings and may be reduced by any earnings during the overall period of unemployment, in accordance with state law. Benefits are not directly conditioned on need. Over a half million beneficiaries will be aided this year.

A

Authorization: Title II of the Emergency Jobs and Unemployment Assistance Act of 1974, as amended.

Budget Code: 16-0179-0-1-504, 16-0326-0-1-603

Catalog Code: 17.225

FY77 Expenditure (est.)

$691 million

Includes 6% for state administration and other support.

TRADE ADJUSTMENT ASSISTANCE-WORKERS

Bureau of International Labor Affairs, Department of Labor

Unemployed and underemployed workers, adversely affected by increased imports competitive with articles they normally produce, are provided weekly cash payments to supplement their regular unemployment insurance benefits, as well as testing, counseling, training, job placement, and job search and relocation allowance. Benefits are in kind and in cash, funded by direct Federal payments, without restrictions on their use. Payments may be up to 70 percent of the beneficiary's average weekly wage, but not more than the national average weekly wage in manufacturing. As many as a half million workers may receive benefits this year. Benefits are not directly conditioned on need.

B

Authorization: Title II of the Trade Act of 1974, PL93-618, 19 USC 2271-2322.

Budget Code: 16-0326-0-1-603

Catalog Code: 17.400

FY77 Expenditure (est.)

$254 million

Includes 6% for state administration and other support.

ECONOMIC ADJUSTMENT ASSISTANCE

Economic Development Administration, Department of Commerce

Assistance is provided to unemployed workers and those threatened with unemployment in state and local areas affected by economic dislocation due to natural disasters, closings of major employers, and international trade agreements. Project grants may be used for rent and mortgage assistance, relocation, unemployment compensation and training, as well as the more generic projects like public facilities and services. Local matching of 25 percent, cash or in kind, is required. About 50 areas are assisted each year. Benefits are conditioned, in part, on need.

C

Authorization: Title IX of the Public Works and Economic Development Act of 1965, PL89-136, as amended by PL93-423, 42 USC 3241, 3243-3245.

Budget Code: 13-2050-0-1-452

Catalog Code: 11.307

FY77 Expenditure (est.)

$30 million

EMERGENCY LOANS

Farmers Home Administration, Department of Agriculture

Farmers, ranchers and aquaculture operators who suffer losses because of a natural disaster are provided renewable, seven-year loans at from one to five percent interest to repair and replace damaged or destroyed property and supplies and to replace income lost due to reduced production of crops and livestock. Other loans to cover operating expenses and essential needs are provided at a market rate of interest when credit is not otherwise available. In both cases, repayment terms vary with the reasonable repayment ability of the borrower. Benefits are in the form of favorable credit terms, funded by the Agricultural Credit Insurance Fund. The appropriation language makes funds available in such amounts as may be necessary each year. Almost 35,000 loans are projected for this year. Benefits are not directly conditioned on need.

C

Authorization: Sections 321-328 of the Consolidated Farm and Rural Development Act, PL92-419, as amended by PL94-68, 7 USC 1961-1968.

Budget Code: 12-4140-0-3-351

Catalog Code: 10.404

FY77 Expenditure (est.)

-negative-

The Agricultural Credit Insurance Fund's capital outlays and operating expenses in FY77 are to be more than offset by receipts, including repayments, interest revenue, sales and beneficial ownership certificates. Estimated FY77 loan commitments are $1 billion.

FEDERAL CROP INSURANCE

Federal Crop Insurance Corporation, Agricultural Stabilization and Conservation Service, Department of Agriculture

Agricultural producers are provided protection from crop losses caused by natural hazards, such as insect and wildlife damage, plant diseases, fire, drought, flood, wind and other weather conditions. Benefits are in the form of low-cost insurance, funded by U.S. Treasury capital stock and by the premiums paid by producers to the Federal Crop Insurance Corporation Fund. Many of the costs of loss adjustment, administration, and operation are not provided for in the premiums but through transfers from general revenues. Almost $2 billion in insurance is in force, covering 320,000 crops on 23 million acres in 1,500 counties. Benefits are not conditioned on need.

C

Authorization: Federal Crop Insurance Act, as amended, 7 USC 1501-1520.

Budget Code: 12-2707-0-1-351, 12-4085-0-3-351

Catalog Code: 10.450

FY77 Expenditure (est.)

$67 million

Represents the FY77 expenses of indemnities, claims, operations and administration, less income from premiums.

CRIME/RIOT INSURANCE

Federal Insurance Administration, Department of Housing & Urban Development

Urban property owners and businessmen are provided: (1) reasonable access to basic property insurance (fire, extended coverage, vandalism) and riot insurance under a cooperative effort of insurance companies, state and Federal government; (2) burglary and robbery insurance at affordable rates for properties that meet protective device requirements. Benefits are in the form of favorable insurance rates, funded by Federal reinsurance against catastrophic loss and Federal underwriting. Over 4 million riot insurance policies have been issued and $19 billion of insurance is in force. Some 30,000 crime insurance policies have been issued. Benefits are not conditioned on need.

C

Authorization: Urban Property Protection and Reinsurance Act of 1968, as amended, Housing and Urban Development Act of 1970, as amended, 12 USC 1749bbb *et seq.*

Budget Code: 86-4235-0-3-403

Catalog Code: 14.002, 14.003

FY77 Expenditure (est.)

$2 million

Represents the FY77 expenses of claims, operations and administration, less income from investment interest and reinsurance receipts.

FARM OPERATING LOANS

Farmers Home Administration, Department of Agriculture

Farmers and ranchers with not-larger-than-family operations are provided renewable operating loans for up to seven years, to be used for a variety of essential farm expenses, as well as for meeting family subsistence needs, purchasing home equipment, refinancing debt, and paying rent and property taxes. Loans are made when credit at reasonable terms is not otherwise available. Benefits are in the form of management assistance and favorable credit terms, funded by the Agricultural Credit Insurance Fund, at an interest rate based on the average rate paid by the U.S. Treasury on obligations of similar maturity. Over 45,000 operating loans are made annually, and the average loan is about $18,000. Benefits are not conditioned on need.

C

Authorization: Title III of the Agricultural Act of 1961, PL87-128, and Title I of the Consolidated Farm and Rural Development Act, PL92-419, 7 USC 1942.

Budget Code: 12-4140-0-3-351

Catalog Code: 10.406

FY77 Expenditure (est.)

-negative-

The Agricultural Credit Insurance Fund's capital outlays and operating expenses in FY77 are to be more than offset by receipts, including repayments, interest revenue, sales of beneficial ownership certificates. Estimated FY77 loan commitments are $610 million.

II. Supplementing Family Earned Income

DAIRY AND BEEKEEPER INDEMNITY PAYMENTS

Agricultural Stabilization and Conservation Service, Department of Agriculture

Indemnity payments are provided to: (1) dairy farmers and dairy product manufacturers who have been directed to remove their milk or milk products from commercial markets because they contain harmful chemical residues; (2) beekeepers who have suffered losses of honeybees because of the nearby use of pesticides and other chemicals. Benefits are in the form of direct cash payments, without restriction on their use, based on the market value of the loss of the milk or dairy products and the replacement cost of the honeybees. Payments to beekeepers average slightly over $3,000. About 1,000 beekeepers and 20 dairy farmers make claims annually. Benefits are not directly conditioned on need.

C

Authorization: Titles II and VIII of the Agricultural Act of 1970, PL91-524, as amended by PL93-86, 7 USC 135b, 450j-1.

Budget Code: 12-3314-0-1-351

Catalog Code: 10.053, 10.060

FY77 Expenditure (est.)

$4 million

COTTON PRODUCTION STABILIZATION PAYMENTS

Agricultural Stabilization and Conservation Service, Department of Agriculture

Owners, tenants and sharecroppers producing cotton are provided guaranteed incomes from that portion of their crops grown on acreage allotments. Benefits are in the form of federally financed direct cash payments, without restrictions on their use, based either on the difference between the average market price and a higher, government-established target price (deficiency payments) or on the loss incurred due to natural disasters which prevented any planting or the harvesting of at least two thirds of the normal allotment crop (disaster payments). The number of participating farms receiving payments varies from year to year depending on conditions. Last year, 55,000 farms received an average of $2,000 each. (No person may receive more than $20,000 in one crop year from any combination of cotton, feed grain and wheat payments.) Benefits are not directly conditioned on need.

C

Authorization: Food and Agriculture Act of 1965, PL89-321, as amended by PL90-559, PL91-524, and PL93-86, 7 USC 1341-1350.

Budget Code: 12-3300-0-1-351, 12-4336-0-3-351

Catalog Code: 10.052

FY77 Expenditure (est.)

$108 million

Adjusted for effects of adverse growing conditions.

FEED GRAIN PRODUCTION STABILIZATION PAYMENTS

Agricultural Stabilization and Conservation Service, Department of Agriculture

Owners, tenants and sharecroppers producing feed grain are provided guaranteed incomes from that portion of their crops grown on acreage allotments. Benefits are in the form of federally financed direct cash payments, without restrictions on their use, based either on the difference between the average market price and a higher, government-established target price (deficiency payments), or on the loss incurred due to natural disasters which prevented any planting or the harvesting of at least two thirds of the normal allotment crop (disaster payments). The number of participating farms receiving payments varies from year to year depending on conditions. Last year, 100,000 farms received an average of $1,100 each. (No person may receive more than $20,000 in one crop year from any combination of cotton, feed grain and wheat payments.) Benefits are not directly conditioned on need.

C

Authorization: Food and Agriculture Act of 1965, PL89-321, as amended by PL90-559, PL91-524, and PL93-86, 7 USC 1421, 1441-42.

Budget Code: 12-4336-0-3-351, 12-3300-0-1-351

Catalog Code: 10.055

FY77 Expenditure (est.)

$228 million

RICE PRODUCTION STABILIZATION PAYMENTS

Agricultural Stabilization and Conservation Service, Department of Agriculture

Owners, tenants and sharecroppers producing rice are provided guaranteed incomes from that portion of their crops grown on acreage allotments. Benefits are in the form of federally financed direct cash payments, without restrictions on their use, based either on the difference between the average market price and a higher, government-established target price (deficiency payments), or on the loss incurred due to natural disasters which prevented any planting or the harvesting of at least two thirds of the normal allotment crop (disaster payments). (No person may receive more than $55,000 in one crop year from any combination of payments that includes a rice payment.) Benefits are not directly conditioned on need.

C

Authorization: Rice Production Act of 1975, PL94-214, 7 USC 428c.

Budget Code: 12-4336-0-3-351, 12-3300-0-1-351

Catalog Code: 10.065

FY77 Expenditure (est.)

$135 million

WHEAT PRODUCTION STABILIZATION PAYMENTS

Agricultural Stabilization and Conservation Service, Department of Agriculture

Owners, tenants and sharecroppers producing wheat are provided guaranteed incomes from that portion of their crops grown on acreage allotments. Benefits are in the form of federally financed direct cash payments, without restrictions on their use, based either on the difference between the average market price and a higher, government-established target price (deficiency payments), or on the loss incurred due to natural disasters which prevented any planting or the harvesting of at least two thirds of the normal allotment crop (disaster payments). The number of participating farms receiving payments varies from year to year depending on conditions. Last year, some 45,000 farms received an average of $1,300 each. (No person may receive more than $20,000 in one crop year from any combination of cotton, feed grain and wheat payments.) Benefits are not directly conditioned on need.

C

Authorization: Food and Agriculture Act of 1965, PL89-321, as amended by PL90-559, PL91-524, and PL93-86, 7 USC 1331-1340, 1379.

Budget Code: 12-4336-0-3-351, 12-3300-0-1-351

Catalog Code: 10.058

FY77 Expenditure (est.)

$111 million

WOOL AND MOHAIR PAYMENTS

Agricultural Stabilization and Conservation Service, Department of Agriculture

Persons owning sheep or lambs and selling shorn wool or unshorn lambs, as well as persons owning angora goats and selling mohair, are provided guaranteed incomes from their wool and mohair production. Benefits are in the form of federally financed direct cash payments, without restrictions on their use, based on the difference between the average market price and a higher, government-established support price. Total nationwide payments are subject to a limitation of 70 percent of gross receipts from import duties on wool and wool manufactures. Benefits are not conditioned on need.

C

Authorization: National Wool Act of 1954, as amended by PL89-321, PL90-559, PL91-524, and PL93-86, 7 USC 1781-1787.

Budget Code: 12-4336-0-3-351, 12-3300-0-1-351

Catalog Code: 10.059

FY77 Expenditure (est.)

$8 million

EARNED INCOME CREDIT

Internal Revenue Service, Department of Treasury

Indirect and direct financial assistance is provided to low-income workers who have dependent children. Benefits are in the form of tax relief and direct cash payments, funded by allowing the workers a credit against tax liability on certain amounts of earned income. The credit reaches a maximum at 10 percent of the first $4,000 of earnings; it is then reduced by 10 percent of all earnings above $4,000, thus phasing out at $8,000 of earnings (or adjusted gross income). Any credit in excess of tax liability is paid in cash to the worker. Over 80 percent of aggregate credits are returned as cash payments. Benefits are conditioned on need.

A

Authorization: Section 43 of the Internal Revenue Code of 1954, as amended by the Tax Reduction Act of 1975 and the Tax Reform Act of 1976.

Budget Code: 20-0903-0-1-604

Catalog Code: none

FY77 Expenditure (est.)

$1,070 million

Represents estimated FY77 revenue loss of $215 million and direct outlays of $856 million.

EXCESS OF PERCENTAGE STANDARD DEDUCTION OVER LOW-INCOME ALLOWANCE

Internal Revenue Service, Department of Treasury

Indirect financial assistance is provided to taxpayers who claim the standard deduction instead of itemizing deductions. The standard deduction is calculated as a percentage of adjusted gross income, but it is subject to a minimum amount, called the low-income allowance. (The total of the low-income allowance and personal exemptions approximates the poverty level and represents a floor below which income is not taxed.) To the extent that one's standard deduction exceeds the low-income allowance, it is being used in lieu of individually itemized deductions. Thus, benefits are in the form of tax relief, funded by allowing the taxpayer to deduct a standard 16 percent of income, up to a maximum based on filing status. Benefits are not directly conditioned on need.

B

Authorization: Section 141 of the Internal Revenue Code of 1954, as amended.

Budget Code: none

Catalog Code: none

FY77 Expenditure (est.)

$1,285 million

Represents estimated FY77 revenue loss. About 1% of such tax expenditures go to tax filers with adjusted gross incomes under $7,000; and 56%, to those between $7,000 and $15,000.

CREDIT FOR CHILD AND DEPENDENT CARE EXPENSES

Internal Revenue Service, Department of Treasury

Indirect financial assistance is provided to taxpayers who must purchase child or dependent care services in order to work or to go to school. Benefits are in the form of tax relief, funded by allowing such taxpayers a credit of 20 percent of eligible expenditures up to certain limits, against tax liability. The credit cannot exceed $2,000 for one dependent and $4,000 for two or more. The credit may be claimed by a divorced or separated parent with custody of a child, and by married couples, if one spouse is disabled, or both are employed full-time or one is employed full-time and the other is a part-time worker or a student. Benefits are not conditioned on need.

B

Authorization: Section 214 of the Internal Revenue Code of 1954, as amended by the Tax Reform Act of 1976.

Budget Code: none

Catalog Code: none

FY77 Expenditure (est.)

$840 million

Represents estimated FY77 revenue loss. Under former provisions, about 4% of such tax expenditures went to tax filers with adjusted gross incomes under $7,000; and 50%, to those between $7,000 and $15,000.

EXCLUSION OF EMPLOYER-FURNISHED MEALS AND LODGING

Internal Revenue Service, Department of Treasury

Indirect financial assistance is provided to employed taxpayers for whom in-kind meals and lodging constitute a portion of their compensation. Benefits are in the form of tax relief, funded by allowing employees to exclude from consideration as income the value of meals and lodging furnished by the employer on his business premises and for his convenience. (Lodging must also be required as a condition of employment.) Live-in housekeepers, resident apartment-house managers, and clergymen's housing allowances are covered under this. Benefits are not conditioned on need.

B

Authorization: Section 119 of the Internal Revenue Code of 1954, as amended.

Budget Code: none

Catalog Code: none

FY77 Expenditure (est.)

$330 million

Represents estimated FY77 revenue loss. About 7% of such tax expenditures go to tax filers with adjusted gross incomes under $7,000; and 32%, to those between $7,000 and $15,000.

EXCLUSION OF EMPLOYER CONTRIBUTIONS TO GROUP TERM LIFE INSURANCE PREMIUMS

Internal Revenue Service, Department of Treasury

Indirect financial assistance is provided to employed taxpayers to help pay for the cost of their group term life insurance. Benefits are in the form of tax relief, funded by allowing employees to exclude from consideration as income the contributions on their behalf by their employers to such insurance plans for coverage up to $50,000. Thus, employers can provide the coverage at less cost than if they had to pay taxable wages sufficient to meet the required premiums. Benefits are not conditioned on need.

B

Authorization: Section 79 of the Internal Revenue Code of 1954, as amended.

Budget Code: none

Catalog Code: none

FY77 Expenditure (est.)

$800 million

Represents estimated FY77 revenue loss. About 7% of such tax expenditures go to tax filers with adjusted gross income under $7,000; and 32%, to those between $7,000 and $15,000.

EXCLUSION OF EMPLOYER CONTRIBUTIONS TO PENSION AND PROFIT-SHARING PLANS

Internal Revenue Service, Department of Treasury

Indirect financial assistance is provided to employed taxpayers to help pay for the cost of maintaining pension and profit-sharing plans on their behalf. Benefits are in the form of tax relief, funded by allowing the employees to exclude from consideration as income the contributions on their behalf by their employers into qualified plans. The earnings of such plans are also non-taxable as they accrue. Thus, employers can provide retirement coverages at less cost than if they had to pay taxable wages sufficient for their employees' purchase of such coverage. Benefits are not conditioned on need.

B

Authorization: Sections 401-407, 410-415 of the Internal Revenue Code of 1954, as amended.

Budget Code: none

Catalog Code: none

FY77 Expenditure (est.)

$8,715 million

Represents estimated FY77 revenue loss. About 4% of such tax expenditures go to tax filers with adjusted gross incomes under $7,000; and 23%, to those between $7,000 and $15,000.

EXCLUSION OF EMPLOYER CONTRIBUTIONS TO ACCIDENT INSURANCE PREMIUMS

Internal Revenue Service, Department of Treasury

Indirect financial assistance is provided to employed taxpayers to help pay for the cost of their accident insurance. Benefits are in the form of tax relief, funded by allowing employees to exclude from consideration as income the contributions on their behalf by their employers to insurance plans covering accidents and accidental death. Thus, employers can provide the coverage at less cost than if they had to pay taxable wages sufficient to meet the required premiums. Benefits are not conditioned on need.

B

Authorization: Section 106 of the Internal Revenue Code of 1954, as amended.

Budget Code: none

Catalog Code: none

FY77 Expenditure (est.)

$70 million

Represents estimated FY77 revenue loss. About 8% of such tax expenditures go to tax filers with adjusted gross incomes under $7,000; and 33%, to those between $7,000 and $15,000.

EXCLUSION OF EMPLOYER CONTRIBUTIONS TO MEDICAL INSURANCE PREMIUMS

Internal Revenue Service, Department of Treasury

Indirect financial assistance is provided to employed taxpayers to help pay for the cost of their health insurance. Benefits are in the form of tax relief, funded by allowing employees to exclude from consideration as income the contributions on their behalf by their employers to insurance plans covering sickness and injury. Thus, employers can provide the coverage at less cost than if they had to pay taxable wages sufficient to meet the required premiums. Benefits are not conditioned on need.

B

Authorization: Section 106 of the Internal Revenue Code of 1954, as amended.

Budget Code: none

Catalog Code: none

FY77 Expenditure (est.)

$5,195 million

Represents estimated FY77 revenue loss. About 8% of such tax expenditures go to tax filers with adjusted gross incomes under $7,000; and 32%, to those between $7,000 and $15,000.

II. Supplementing Family Earned Income

PUBLIC SERVICE EMPLOYMENT

Employment and Training Administration, Department of Labor

Unemployed and underemployed persons, generally in areas of substantial unemployment, are provided jobs in local public services. Preference is given to the disadvantaged, to the long-term unemployed, and to those who have exhausted, or were not eligible for, unemployment insurance. Benefits are in the form of cash compensation for work performed, funded by formula grants based on the number and percentage of unemployed in each state and locality of 100,000 population. The grants are used to finance the salaries, wages, and benefits of workers hired under the program. Generally, compensation is equivalent to that of the private-sector for similar work, subject to certain maximums. About 600,000 persons are employed in these positions. Benefits may be conditioned, in part, on need.

B

Authorization: Titles I, II, and VI of the Comprehensive Employment and Training Act of 1973, PL93-203, as amended by the Emergency Jobs and Unemployment Assistance Act of 1974, PL93-567.

Budget Code: 16-0173-0-1-504, 16-0174-0-1-504

Catalog Code: 17.232

FY77 Expenditure (est.)

$3,159 million

Includes approximately 5% for local and state administration and other support.

ECONOMIC OPPORTUNITY LOANS

Small Business Administration

Low-income and socially disadvantaged persons denied normal access to credit are provided management assistance and 15-year loans at 7.6 percent, of up to $100,000 for the purpose of establishing, preserving and strengthening certain types of small business. The management training is made an integral part of the loan program. Benefits are in the form of favorable credit and collateral terms, funded by direct, immediate-participation or guaranteed loans. About 1,000 direct and immediate-participation loans are made annually, and about 500 loans are guaranteed. To date, some $270 million in direct and participation loans is outstanding, and about $90 million in loans is guaranteed. Benefits are conditioned, in part, on need.

C

Authorization: Section 7(i) of the Small Business Act, PL85-536, as amended, 15 USC 636(I), PL93-386.

Budget Code: 73-4154-0-3-403

Catalog Code: 59.003

FY77 Expenditure (est.)

$50 million

Loan fund capital outlays and operating expenses in FY77 are partially offset by receipts, including repayments, recoveries and interest revenue. Estimated FY77 loan commitments are $70 million.

FARM OWNERSHIP LOANS

Farmers Home Administration, Department of Agriculture

Farmers and ranchers with not-larger-than-family operations are provided 40-year loans at five percent interest to acquire, enlarge and improve farms, to accomplish related purposes, to refinance debt and to construct or repair farmhouses and farm service buildings. Loans are made when credit at reasonable terms is not otherwise available. Benefits are in the form of favorable credit terms, funded by the Agricultural Credit Insurance Fund. Management assistance is provided as needed to enable families to become successfully established. About 11,000 loans are made annually and the average loan is about $42,000. Benefits are not conditioned on need.

C

Authorization: Section 302 of the Consolidated Farm and Rural Development Act, PL92-419, 7 USC 1922.

Budget Code: 12-4140-0-3-351

Catalog Code: 10.407

FY77 Expenditure (est.)

-negative-

The Agricultural Credit Insurance Fund's capital outlays and operating expenses in FY77 are to be more than offset by receipts, including repayments, interest revenue, and sales of beneficial ownership certificates. Estimated FY77 loan commitments are $450 million.

SUMMER YOUTH EMPLOYMENT

Employment and Training Administration, Department of Labor

Economically disadvantaged youths, aged 14-21, are provided jobs during the summer months. Benefits are in the form of cash compensation, funded by formula grants to 400 local and state prime sponsors. Approximately 800,000 youths are employed each summer in a variety of make-work slots in their communities, in government agencies and in nonprofit organizations. The youths earn $2.30 per hour and generally work 24 hours weekly for seven weeks. Benefits are conditioned on need; the operation is more that of an income maintenance program than a work experience or public works program.

A

Authorization: Section 304(a) (3) of the Comprehensive Employment and Training Act of 1973, PL93-203, as amended.

Budget Code: 16-0174-0-1-504

Catalog Code: 17.232

FY77 Expenditures (est.)

$595 million

Includes under 10% for state and local administration and other support.

III
PROGRAMS PROVIDING BENEFITS TO SUPPLEMENT THE GENERAL INCOME OF THE FAMILY

EMERGENCY ASSISTANCE TO NEEDY FAMILIES WITH CHILDREN

Social and Rehabilitation Service, Department of Health, Education & Welfare

Emergency public assistance is provided to needy families with children in order to prevent destitution or to provide living arrangements for families without available resources. Assistance may not be granted for longer than 30 days in a 12-month period. Benefits may be in cash, in kind, or in voucher form, provided directly to the family in amounts varying according to the family's income and needs as determined under state law. (About three fifths of the states have elected to operate this program.) Benefits are funded by formula grants to state welfare agencies requiring 50-percent matching. Each month, on the average, about 110,000 recipients in 30,000 families are aided. Benefits are conditioned on need.

A

Authorization: Title IV-A of the Social Security Act, as amended, 42 USC 601 *et seq.*

Budget Code: 75-0581-0-1-999

Catalog Code: 13.761

FY77 Expenditure (est.)

$60 million

Includes over 10% for state and local administration and other support.

INDOCHINESE REFUGEE ASSISTANCE

Social and Rehabilitation Service, Department of Health, Education & Welfare

Recent refugees in alien status from Cambodia, Laos, and Vietnam are provided public assistance, medical assistance, and other welfare services for the needy, as well as a small amount of other social services. Benefits are both in cash (public assistance) and in kind, funded by 100-percent Federal grants to state welfare agencies. The enabling legislation for this program expires during 1977, after which time needy refugees will be assisted through existing programs for the entire population. Benefits are conditioned on need.

A

Authorization: The Indochina Migration and Refugee Assistance Act of 1975, PL94-23, as amended by PL94-313.

Budget Code: 75-0570-0-1-604

Catalog Code: 13.769

FY77 Expenditure (est.)

$95 million

Includes over 10% for state and local administration and other support.

CUBAN REFUGEE ASSISTANCE

Social and Rehabilitation Service, Department of Health, Education & Welfare

Cuban refugees in alien status registered with the Cuban Refugee Center in Miami, Florida are provided public assistance, medical assistance and other welfare services for the needy, as well as a small amount of other social services. Benefits are both in cash (public assistance) and in kind, funded by 100-percent Federal grants to state welfare agencies and to the refugee center in Miami. Less than 70,000 Cuban refugees nationwide receive public assistance and/or medical assistance. This program will gradually be phased out and integrated into existing programs serving the entire population. Benefits are conditioned on need.

A

Authorization: Migration and Refugee Assistance Act of 1962, PL87-510, 22 USC 2601-2605.

Budget Code: 75-0573-0-1-604

Catalog Code: 13.762

FY77 Expenditure (est.)

$68 million

Includes over 10% for state and local administration and other support.

INDIAN GENERAL ASSISTANCE

Bureau of Indian Affairs, Department of Interior

Maintenance payments to cover the costs of food, shelter, clothing, and other items of daily living are made to needy Indians living on or near reservations, when such assistance is not available from state or local agencies. Benefits are in the form of cash, in amounts depending upon family size and needs, and without restrictions on use. Each month, on the average, some 65,000 Indians receive cash assistance. Benefits are conditioned on need.

A

Authorization: Snyder Act of 1921, PL67-85, 25 USC 13.

Budget Code: 14-2100-0-1-999

Catalog Code: 15.133

FY77 Expenditure (est.)

$64 million

VETERANS LIFE INSURANCE

Department of Veterans Benefits, Veterans Administration

Non-dishonorably discharged veterans of both World Wars and the Korean conflict, as well as service-disabled veterans of the Vietnam conflict, are provided life insurance protection, settlement upon death, cash surrender of a policy if desired, loans of up to 94 percent of the cash surrender value, and dividends on some policies. Benefits are in the form of cash (settlements, cash surrenders, dividends, loans) and in the form of favorable insurance terms. (In some funds, premiums do not cover operating and capital reserve requirements, and deficits are met by transfers from other funds.) Five insurance funds are financed from premiums, interest on investments, and, for some, payments or transfers from appropriations and other accounts. Approximately five million policies are in effect, and annual payments comprise about $430 million to beneficiaries and $530 million to policyholders. Benefits are not conditioned on need.

C

Authorization: War Risk Insurance Act of 1917, PL65-90; National Service Life Insurance Act of 1940, PL76-801; PL82-23; PL85-896; PL88-664; PL92-95, and PL92-193; 38 USC 701, 722, 723, 725, 740, and 806.

Budget Code: 36-4010-0-3-701, 36-4012-0-3-701, 36-8132-0-7-701, 36-8150-0-7-701, 36-8455-0-8-701

Catalog Code: 64.103

FY77 Expenditure (est.)

$648 million

Represents FY77 program costs (about $1.2 billion), less income from loan repayments, premiums, interest, settlements, and transfers and appropriations.

EXCLUSION OF INTEREST ON LIFE INSURANCE SAVINGS

Internal Revenue Service, Department of Treasury

Indirect financial assistance is provided to taxpayers who purchase life insurance policies that accumulate interest-bearing reserves. Benefits are in the form of tax relief, funded by allowing the policyholder to exclude from consideration as income the annual interest earned on the accumulated reserves. In effect, this reduces the policyholder's premiums, allowing the insurance to be purchased with tax-free interest income. Benefits are not conditioned on need.

C

Authorization: Section 101(a) of the Internal Revenue Code of 1954, as amended, and Section 1.451-2 of the Income Tax Regulations.

Budget Code: none

Catalog Code: none

FY77 Expenditure (est.)

$1,815 million

Represents estimated FY77 revenue loss. About 11% of such tax expenditures go to tax filers with adjusted gross incomes under $7,000; and 23%, to those between $7,000 and $15,000.

DISASTER ASSISTANCE

Federal Disaster Assistance Administration, Department of Housing & Urban Development

Individual disaster victims in declared emergency and major disaster areas are provided shelter and temporary housing if displaced, assistance if put out of work, emergency transportation service, food coupons, grants to meet disaster-related expenses, and crisis counseling. Benefits are mainly in kind, funded by project grants to affected state and local governments and by the provision of Federal facilities, equipment and personnel. A substantial portion of the funds is used for repair and replacement of public facilities, for removal of wreckage and debris, and for essential work on public lands. No matching contribution is required, except for family and individual grant programs. Benefits are conditioned, in part, on need.

C

Authorization: Disaster Relief Act of 1970, PL91-606; Disaster Relief Act of 1974, PL93-288; Executive Orders 11749, 11795.

Budget Code: 11-0039-1-453, 86-3981-0-4-453

Catalog Code: 14.701

FY77 Expenditure (est.)

$387 million

PHYSICAL DISASTER LOANS

Small Business Administration

Owners of property damaged or destroyed by natural disasters in designated areas are provided 30-year loans at 6.6 percent, regardless of the availability of credit from other sources or a borrower's own ability to provide the needed funds. Loans may be used for repair or replacement of realty, machinery, equipment, household and other personal property, but not for agricultural purposes. Benefits are in the form of favorable credit terms, funded by direct and immediate participation loans. No local funding is required. To date, well over a half million disaster loans, totalling almost $4 billion, have been approved. Benefits are not conditioned on need.

C

Authorization: Section 7(b) of the Small Business Act, PL85-536, as amended, 15 USC 636(B); Disaster Relief Act of 1970, PL91-606, 42 USC 4401; PL93-24, PL94-68.

Budget Code: 73-4153-0-3-453

Catalog Code: 59.008

FY77 Expenditure (est.)

$86 million

Loan fund capital outlays and operating expenses in FY77 are to be partially offset by receipts from repayments, recoveries, interest revenue, etc. Estimated FY77 loan commitments are $137 million.

FLOOD INSURANCE

Federal Insurance Administration, Department of Housing & Urban Development

Property owners in communities which have entered into the National Flood Insurance Program are provided flood insurance at a premium rate which is lower than a normal actuarial rate. The coverage maximum for a single-family home and for its contents is $90,000. Benefits are in the form of favorable insurance rates, funded by a Federal subsidy of the program which is a cooperative venture with the private insurance industry. Almost 1.2 million policies are in force in some 16,000 communities nationwide, for a total insurance of $33 billion. Benefits are not conditioned on need.

C

Authorization: National Flood Insurance Act of 1968, PL90-448, as amended by the Flood Disaster Protection Act of 1973, PL93-324, 42 USC 4011, 4021, 4056, 4127.

Budget Code: 86-4236-0-3-453

Catalog Code: 14.001

FY77 Expenditure (est.)

$178 million

Represents the FY77 expenses of underwriting, loss and adjustment, interest, studies and land surveys, and administration, less nominal reinsurance receipts.

DEDUCTIBILITY OF CASUALTY LOSSES

Internal Revenue Service, Department of Treasury

Indirect financial assistance is provided to taxpayers who suffer losses attributable to theft, fire, shipwreck or other casualties. Benefits are in the form of tax relief, funded by allowing the property owner to deduct the value of casualty losses in excess of insurance recoveries from gross income. In effect, this shifts the burden of loss partly away from the property owner to the general taxpayer. This provision applies only to personal income tax liability and not to corporations. Benefits are not conditioned on need.

C

Authorization: Section 165(c)(3) of the Internal Revenue Code of 1954, as amended.

Budget Code: none

Catalog Code: none

FY77 Expenditure (est.)

$345 million

Represents estimated FY77 revenue loss. About 3% of such tax expenditures go to tax filers with adjusted gross incomes under $7,000; and 28%, to those between $7,000 and $15,000.

CRIPPLED CHILDREN'S SERVICES

Health Services Administration, Department of Health, Education & Welfare

Physician services, including medical, surgical, corrective, diagnostic and after-care services and hospitalization, are provided to children under 21 years of age who are crippled or suffering from conditions that lead to crippling. Benefits are in kind, funded by grants to appropriate state agencies which purchase appropriate services and care from hospitals and other providers. State matching of formula grants is required on a dollar-for-dollar basis. Over a half million crippled children are aided annually, including 100,000 with multiple handicaps. Benefits are not directly conditioned on need.

C

Authorization: Section 504 of the Social Security Act as amended, 42 USC 704.

Budget Code: 75-0350-0-1-551

Catalog Code: 13.211

FY77 Expenditure (est.)

$98 million

FAMILY PLANNING PROJECTS

Health Services Administration, Department of Health, Education & Welfare

Contraceptive advice and supplies and services, including physical examinations, diagnosis and treatment (but excluding abortions) are provided, with priority given to persons from low-income families. Benefits are in kind, funded by project grants to state and local agencies and nonprofit agencies to pay for services to persons who desire them, who would not otherwise have access to them and who are in need. Some local contribution is required toward project cost. Approximately 3,000,000 persons are to receive service this year. Benefits are conditioned, in part, on need.

B

Authorization: Section 1001 of the Public Health Service Act, PL78-410, as amended, 42 USC 300.

Budget Code: 75-0305-0-1-551

Catalog Code: 13.217

FY77 Expenditure (est.)

$121 million

MATERNAL AND CHILD HEALTH SERVICES

Health Services Administration, Department of Health, Education & Welfare

Mothers, infants and school-age children, especially in rural areas or areas with concentrations of low-income families, are provided comprehensive health care services aimed at (a) reducing the incidence of mental retardation and other handicaps caused by complications associated with childbearing; (b) reducing the incidence of infant and maternal mortality; and (c) promoting the medical and dental health of children and youth. Benefits are in kind, funded by grants to state health agencies for the purchase of inpatient care and health services in maternity clinics, well-child and pediatric clinics, special clinics for mentally retarded children, and other facilities. State matching of formula grants is required on a dollar-for-dollar basis. Almost two million children are served in well-child clinics yearly; almost one million receive dental care treatment; and over a half million women and 160,000 infants receive comprehensive prenatal and postpartum health care. Benefits are not directly conditioned on need.

B

Authorization: Section 503 of the Social Security Act, as amended, 42 USC 703.

Budget Code: 75-0350-0-1-551

Catalog Code: 13.232

FY77 Expenditure (est.)

$241 million

MENTAL HEALTH — CHILDREN'S SERVICES

Alcohol, Drug Abuse and Mental Health Administration, Department of Health, Education & Welfare

Mental health services are provided to children and their families by community-based facilities. Benefits are in kind, often social services, funded by staffing grants which meet a portion of the compensation costs of professional and technical staff in the initial operation of 138 community mental health centers, their affiliates, and other nonprofit agencies. The Federal matching percentage is somewhat higher in poverty areas, but the percentage in all areas decreases with each succeeding year. Although open to the general public in the catchment area, benefits are conditioned, in part, on need, because of a sliding-scale fee schedule based on family income.

B

Authorization: Part A, Section 203(d) of the Community Mental Health Centers Amendments of 1975, PL94-63.

Budget Code: 75-1361-0-1-550

Catalog Code: 13.259

FY77 Expenditure (est.)

$18 million

COMPREHENSIVE SERVICES SUPPORT

Alcohol, Drug Abuse and Mental Health Administration, Department of Health, Education & Welfare

All persons residing in a catchment area are eligible for comprehensive mental health services, including inpatient, outpatient, day care and emergency services, and partial hospitalization and follow-up care. Special services are provided for children, the elderly, alcohol and drug abusers and residents discharged from state facilities. Benefits are in kind, provided by various types of grants to approximately 300 community facilities and nonprofit agencies, including grants for initial operations, conversion to new services, and financial distress. Poverty areas receive somewhat higher Federal matching shares for several grant types. Although open to the general public in the catchment area, benefits are conditioned, in part, on need, because of a sliding-scale fee schedule based on family income.

B

Authorization: Title III of the Community Mental Health Centers Amendments of 1975, PL94-63, 42 USC 2681-2696.

Budget Code: 75-1361-0-1-550

Catalog Code: 13.295

FY77 Expenditure (est.)

$132 million

DRUG ABUSE COMMUNITY SERVICE PROGRAMS

Alcohol, Drug Abuse and Mental Health Administration, Department of Health, Education & Welfare

Narcotics addicts, drug abusers and drug-dependent persons are provided inpatient, outpatient, residential, emergency and after-care services in community-based facilities. Benefits are in kind, funded by grants to community mental health centers, their affiliates and other nonprofit agencies. Staffing grants meet a portion of the compensation costs of professional and technical personnel. Project grants may meet a portion of operating costs. The Federal matching percentage is somewhat higher in poverty areas, but the percentage in all areas decreases with each succeeding year. The goal is 100,000 treatment slots. Although open to the general public in the catchment area, benefits are conditioned, in part, on need, because of a sliding-scale fee schedule based on family income.

B

Authorization: Part A, Section 203(e) of the Community Mental Health Centers Amendments of 1975, PL94-63; Section 410 of the Drug Abuse Office and Treatment Act of 1972, PL92-255 as amended by PL94-237.

Budget Code: 75-1361-0-1-550

Catalog Code: 13.235

FY77 Expenditure (est.)

$159 million

133

VETERANS REHABILITATION — ALCOHOL AND DRUG DEPENDENCE

Department of Medicine and Surgery, Veterans Administration

Alcohol- and drug-dependent veterans discharged or released from active service under conditions other than dishonorable, are provided mental, social, psychiatric, and vocational rehabilitation services. Benefits are in kind, funded principally by means of the salaries and expenses of personnel assigned to VA hospitals and VA outpatient clinics. About 80 alcohol dependence and 50 drug dependence programs are operated by the VA. Benefits are not conditioned on need.

B

Authorization: 38 USC Chapter 17.

Budget Code: 36-0160-0-1-703

Catalog Code: 64.019

FY77 Expenditure (est.)

$107 million

134

ALCOHOL COMMUNITY SERVICE PROGRAMS

Alcohol, Drug Abuse and Mental Health Administration, Department of Health, Education & Welfare

Alcoholics and problem drinkers are provided inpatient, outpatient, residential, emergency and after-care services in community-based facilities. Benefits are in kind, funded by grants to community mental health centers, their affiliates and other nonprofit agencies. Staffing grants meet a portion of the compensation costs of professional and technical staff in the initial operation of the facility. The Federal matching percentage is somewhat higher in poverty areas, but the percentage in all areas decreases with each succeeding year. About 50 programs are to be supported this year. Although open to the general public in the catchment area, benefits are conditioned, in part, on need, because of a sliding-scale fee schedule based on family income.

B

Authorization: Part A, Section 203(e) of the Community Mental Health Centers Amendments of 1975, PL94-63, PL94-371.

Budget Code: 75-1361-0-1-550

Catalog Code: 13.251

FY77 Expenditure (est.)

$56 million

COMMUNITY MENTAL HEALTH CENTERS

Alcohol, Drug Abuse and Mental Health Administration, Department of Health, Education & Welfare

All persons residing in a center's catchment area are eligible for mental health services, including inpatient, outpatient, emergency services and partial hospitalization. Benefits are in kind, funded by staffing grants that meet a portion of the compensation costs of professional and technical staff in the initial operation of the center. The Federal matching percentage is somewhat higher in poverty areas, but the percentage in all areas decreases with each succeeding year. About 280 centers are to be supported this year. Although open to the general public in the catchment area, benefits are conditioned, in part, on need, because of a sliding-scale fee schedule based on family income.

B

Authorization: Title II, Part A of the Mental Retardation Facilities and Community Mental Health Centers Construction Act of 1963, PL88-164, as amended by PL89-105, PL90-31, PL90-574, PL91-211, PL91-513, PL91-515, and PL94-63.

Budget Code: 75-1361-0-1-550

Catalog Code: 13.240

FY77 Expenditure (est.)

$79 million

COMMUNITY HEALTH CENTERS

Health Services Administration, Department of Health, Education & Welfare

Primary ambulatory health care is provided, and special and inpatient care arranged, for people in medically underserved areas, especially urban poverty areas. Benefits are in kind, funded by grants to state and local governments and nonprofit agencies which use the funds for the development and operation of community health centers and for the acquisition and/or modernization of facilities. Local matching is determined on a case-by-case basis. Over 3,000,000 persons annually receive care in 164 community and 258 primary health centers receiving support under this program. Although open to the general public in the catchment area, benefits are conditioned, in part, on need, because of a sliding-scale fee schedule based on family income.

A

Authorization: Section 330 of the Public Health Service Act, as amended by Title V, PL94-63, 42 USC 254C.

Budget Code: 75-0350-0-1-551

Catalog Code: 13.224

FY77 Expenditure (est.)

$229 million

NATIONAL HEALTH SERVICE CORPS

Health Services Administration, Department of Health, Education & Welfare

Persons living in areas with critical shortages of health personnel are provided primary medical and dental care. Benefits are in kind, funded by means of the salaries and expenses of Corps personnel assigned to designated areas. There are no set matching requirements, but localities are encouraged to provide facilities and services. All persons in the area are eligible to receive health services at reasonable cost, but persons determined unable to pay the regular fee may be charged a reduced fee or not charged at all. Approximately 700 Corps personnel serve over 400 communities. Benefits are conditioned, in part, on need.

B

Authorization: Section 329 of the Public Health Service Act, PL78-410, as amended, 42 USC 248.

Budget Code: 75-0350-0-1-551

Catalog Code: 13.258

FY77 Expenditure (est.)

$26 million

INDIAN HEALTH SERVICES

Health Services Administration, Department of Health, Education & Welfare

Primary ambulatory health care and inpatient care are provided American Indians and Alaskan natives. Benefits are in kind, provided directly by Federal facilities, contracted for with private and community facilities, or purchased from private physicians, dentists and other professionals. No local matching is required. Over 100,000 hospital admissions and 2,500,000 outpatient visits are covered in a year. Benefits are not directly conditioned on need.

A

Authorization: PL83-568, 42 USC 2001-2004a; Indian Self-Determination Act, PL93-638, 25 USC 450; PL94-437.

Budget Code: 75-0390-0-1-554

Catalog Code: 13.229

FY77 Expenditure (est.)

$245 million

Excludes $100 million in preventive public health and education programs.

MIGRANT HEALTH GRANTS

Health Services Administration, Department of Health, Education & Welfare

Migratory and seasonal agricultural workers and their families are provided primary health care services, wherever they move and work. Benefits are in kind, funded by contract grants with nonprofit agencies which are to improve the work environment of the beneficiaries and to establish clearly defined migrant health centers. No local contribution is required. About 100 projects are funded annually. Benefits are not directly conditioned on need.

A

Authorization: Section 319 of the Public Health Service Act, PL94-63, 42 USC 242h.

Budget Code: 75-0350-0-1-551

Catalog Code: 13.246

FY77 Expenditure (est.)

$32 million

HEALTH MAINTENANCE ORGANIZATION DEVELOPMENT

Health Services Administration, Department of Health, Education & Welfare

Comprehensive, pre-paid health care is provided to persons living in Health Maintenance Organization service areas. Benefits are in kind, funded by contract grants and direct and guaranteed loans to non-profit agencies. Profit-making agencies in medically underserved areas may also receive such assistance. Local matching of 10 percent is required in all but medically underserved areas. Approximately 30 Health Maintenance Organizations serving 900,000 enrollees are to be brought into operational status this year. This program is meant to subsidize Health Maintenance Organization start-up costs, especially feasibility, planning and development efforts and initial operation. Benefits are not directly conditioned on need.

B

Authorization: Title XIII of the Public Health Service Act, PL78-410, as amended by the Health Maintenance Organization Act of 1973, PL93-222, and by PL94-460, 42 USC 300e.

Budget Code: 75-0305-0-1-551, 75-4435-0-3-551

Catalog Code: 13.256

FY77 Expenditure (est.)

$39 million

Most of loan fund capital outlays in FY77 are to be off-set by receipts (interest and loan sales). Estimated FY77 loan commitments are $60 million; grant outlays, $23 million.

COMPREHENSIVE PUBLIC HEALTH SERVICES — FORMULA GRANTS

Health Services Administration, Department of Health, Education & Welfare

Comprehensive public health services, including some primary care in dental and medical clinics, as well as mental health, diagnostic, family planning and nursing services, are provided to both the general populace and high-risk groups. Benefits are in kind, funded by formula grants to state health and mental health agencies. A large portion of this funding is utilized in communicable disease control, environmental health programs and various screening programs for the general populace, as provided by state programs. Benefits are not conditioned on need.

B

Authorization: Section 314(d) of the Public Health Service Act, PL78-410, as amended, 42 USC 246.

Budget Code: 75-0350-0-1-551

Catalog Code: 13.210

FY77 Expenditure (est.)

$95 million

DEDUCTIBILITY OF MEDICAL EXPENSES

Internal Revenue Service, Department of Treasury

Indirect financial assistance is provided to taxpayers to help offset their medical expenses, including the costs of health services, medicine, drugs and health insurance. Benefits are in the form of tax relief, funded by allowing the taxpayer to deduct from gross income the cost of medical services in excess of three percent of income, the cost of medicine and drugs in excess of one percent, and half the cost of medical insurance premiums up to $150 yearly. Benefits are not directly conditioned on need.

B

Authorization: Section 213 of the Internal Revenue Code of 1954, as amended.

Budget Code: none

Catalog Code: none

FY77 Expenditure (est.)

$2,585 million

Represents estimated FY77 revenue loss. About 7% of such tax expenditures go to tax filers with adjusted gross incomes under $7,000; and 35%, to those between $7,000 and $15,000.

SPECIAL SUPPLEMENTAL FOOD PROGRAM (WIC)

Food and Nutrition Service, Department of Agriculture

Nutritious food supplements are provided to pregnant or lactating women, infants and children up to 5 years old, who are determined by competent professionals to be suffering from nutritional deprivation as a result of inadequate nutrition and low income. The WIC package consists of iron-fortified infant formula, milk or cheese, high-iron breakfast cereal and high-vitamin fruit juices. Benefits are in kind, funded by project grants to state health departments for allocation among participating local nonprofit health clinics. Local matching funds are not required. On the average, one million persons receive WIC supplements monthly, and average benefits per person are $22 monthly. Benefits are conditioned on need.

B

Authorization: Child Nutrition Act of 1966, PL89-642, as amended by PL92-433 and PL94-105, 42 USC 1786.

Budget Code: 12-3510-0-1-604

Catalog Code: 10.557

FY77 Expenditure (est.)

$248 million

Includes 20% for project administration.

III. Supplementing Family General Income

FOOD DONATIONS

Food and Nutrition Service, Department of Agriculture

Commodities are provided to needy persons or Indian reservations until their transition to the Food Stamp program, as well as to residents of the Pacific Trust Territories. Also, supplemental food packages are provided to low-income women, infants and children. Distributing agencies receive grants to assist them in meeting expenses. Benefits are in kind, funded by USDA purchase of surplus agricultural commodities which are then distributed free to recipients. Benefits are conditioned on need.

B

Authorization: Section 4(a) of the Agriculture and Consumer Protection Act of 1973, as amended, 7 USC 612(c).

Budget Code: 12-3503-0-1-604

Catalog Code: 10.550

FY77 Expenditure (est.)

$28 million

SCHOOL MILK PROGRAM

Food and Nutrition Service, Department of Agriculture

School children of twelfth grade and under, in public and nonprofit private schools, and in child-care centers, are provided low-cost milk for meals and supplements in school at "full" price or free, according to the family income of each child. Benefits are in kind, funded by formula grants to state educational departments, which in turn allocate the funds among participating schools and institutions. There are no matching requirements, but the cost of milk in excess of Federal reimbursement (6.6 cents per half-pint) must be borne by sources within the state. Well over 2 billion half-pints of milk are served annually. Benefits are conditioned, in part, on need.

A

Authorization: Child Nutrition Act of 1966, PL89-642 as amended by PL91-295, PL93-150, PL93-347, PL94-105, 42 USC 1772.

Budget Code: 12-3502-0-1-604

Catalog Code: 10.556

FY77 Expenditure (est.)

$177 million

NATIONAL SCHOOL LUNCH PROGRAM

Food and Nutrition Service, Department of Agriculture

School children of twelfth grade and under, in participating public and nonprofit private schools, are provided low-cost, nutritional lunches at "full," reduced or no price, according to the family income of each child. Benefits are in kind, funded by formula grants and food donations to state educational departments, which in turn allocate the funds and food among participating schools. State and school district matching on a 3-to-1 basis is required, but schools receive additional assistance for free and reduced-price lunches served. Almost 4.5 billion lunches are served each school year, reaching 27 million children. Almost half the lunches are served at free or reduced prices to low-income children. Benefits are conditioned, in part, on need.

A

Authorization: National School Lunch Act of 1946, PL79-396, as amended by PL87-823, PL91-248, PL92-153, PL92-433, PL93-150, PL93-326, PL94-105, 42 USC 1751-1753.

Budget Code: 12-3539-0-1-604

Catalog Code: 10.555

FY77 Expenditure (est.)

$2,204 million

Includes almost $500 million in distributed commodities.

SCHOOL BREAKFAST PROGRAM

Food and Nutrition Service, Department of Agriculture

School children of twelfth grade and under, in participating public and nonprofit private schools, are provided low-cost, nutritional breakfasts at "full," reduced or no price, according to the family income of each child. Benefits are in kind, funded by formula grants and food donations to state educational departments which in turn allocate the funds and food among participating schools. Local matching funds are not required, but the cost of breakfasts in excess of Federal reimbursement must be borne by sources within the state. Schools receive a higher level of reimbursement for each reduced-price and free breakfast served. About 530 million breakfasts are to be served this school year, reaching 3.5 million children. Benefits are conditioned, in part, on need.

A

Authorization: Child Nutrition Act of 1966, PL89-642, as amended by PL90-301, PL91-248, PL92-32, PL92-433, and PL94-105, 42 USC 1773.

Budget Code: 12-3539-0-1-604

Catalog Code: 10.553

FY77 Expenditure (est.)

$191 million

Includes almost $50 million in distributed commodities.

SUMMER FOOD PROGRAM

Food and Nutrition Service, Department of Agriculture

During the summer months, from May to September, children from low-income areas are provided free breakfasts, lunches, suppers and snacks, or various combinations thereof. Benefits are in kind, funded by formula grants and food donations to state educational departments which in turn allocate the funds and food among participating public and nonprofit private service institutions on the basis of per meal reimbursement. Almost 300 million meals are to be served this summer, reaching 4.5 million children. Benefits are not directly conditioned on individual need.

A

Authorization: Section 13 of the National School Lunch Act as amended by PL94-105.

Budget Code: 12-3539-0-1-604

Catalog Code: 10.559

FY77 Expenditure (est.)

$195 million

Includes approximately $10 million in distributed commodities and 2% for state administration.

CHILD CARE FOOD PROGRAM

Food and Nutrition Service, Department of Agriculture

Preschool children receive low-cost breakfasts, lunches, suppers and snacks, at "full," reduced or no price, according to the family income of each child. Benefits are in kind, funded by formula grants and food donations to state educational departments which, in turn, allocate the funds and food among participating day care centers, settlement houses, Head Start centers, and handicapped day care institutions. Allocations are on the basis of per meal reimbursement. About 351 million meals are served each year, reaching almost 600,000 children. Benefits are conditioned on need.

A

Authorization: Section 17 of the National School Lunch Act of 1946 as amended by PL94-105.

Budget Code: 12-3539-0-1-604

Catalog Code: 10.558

FY77 Expenditure (est.)

$115 million

Includes approximately $10 million in distributed commodities.

COMMUNITY FOOD AND NUTRITION

Community Services Administration

Low-income persons are provided a variety of services, under a plan approved by the local community action (anti-poverty) agency, with the aim of counteracting hunger and malnutrition among the poor. Services vary from nutritional and consumer education to food banks, food vouchers, feeding programs, and food stamp assistance. In all cases, the 100-percent Federal funding is "seed money" for short-term solutions that supplement, broaden or extend assistance provided by the major Federal food and nutrition programs. Benefits are conditioned on need.

A

Authorization: Economic Opportunity Act of 1964, as amended by the Community Services Act of 1974, Section 222A(5) of PL93-644, 42 USC 2809.

Budget Code: 81-0500-0-1-999

Catalog Code: 49.005

FY77 Expenditure (est.)
$29 million

FOOD STAMPS

Food and Nutrition Service, Department of Agriculture

Low-income households are provided increased food-buying power by purchasing food stamps with a face value that exceeds their cost. The stamps may then be used in participating retail food establishments at face value. The difference between the stamps' face value and their cost represents the benefit or "bonus" to a household, and the cost for a given value of stamps varies according to the household's size and adjusted income. Eligibility and benefit standards are national. Benefits may be considered to be in kind, funded by Federal direct payments for a restricted use. States must pay 50 percent of administrative costs. On the average, over 17 million persons participate in the program each month; and the average "bonus" per person is about $24 monthly. Benefits are conditioned on need.

A

Authorization: Food Stamp Act of 1964, PL88-525, as amended by PL90-91, PL90-552, PL91-116, PL91-671, PL92-603, PL93-86, PL93-233, PL93-335, PL93-347, PL93-563, PL94-182, PL94-339, PL94-365, PL94-379, and PL94-585, 7 USC 2011-2025.

Budget Code: 12-3505-0-1-604

Catalog Code: 10.551

FY77 Expenditure (est.)

$5,474 million

Includes 7% for state administration and other support.

152

LOWER INCOME HOUSING ASSISTANCE PAYMENTS

Housing Production and Mortgage Credit, Department of Housing & Urban Development

Low-income families are provided assistance in obtaining decent, safe and sanitary rental housing in existing private accommodations or in newly constructed or substantially rehabilitated housing. Very low-income families pay rents equal to 15 percent of adjusted income; other low-income families (whose incomes are between 50 and 80 percent of the area median) pay rents up to 25 percent of adjusted income. Benefits are in kind, funded by Federal payments to the developers and owners; these payments make up the difference between what the occupants pay for rent and established market rent for the unit. Reservations for approximately 400,000 units to be covered by contract are in effect. Benefits are conditioned on need.

A

Authorization: Section 8 of the Housing Act of 1937, as amended by the Housing and Community Development Act of 1974, PL93-383, 42 USC 1401-1435, 1437F.

Budget Code: 86-0139-0-1-604, 86-0164-0-1-604

Catalog Code: 14.156

FY77 Expenditure (est.)

$362 million

Represents that portion of $1.1 billion authorized for 1977 actually to be spent because of slow program start-up.

RENTAL HOUSING ASSISTANCE AND PAYMENTS

Housing Production and Mortgage Credit, Department of Housing & Urban Development

Low- and moderate-income persons are provided good quality rental and cooperative housing at rents equal to at least 25 percent of adjusted income. Benefits are in kind, funded by monthly interest subsidies to the mortgagee, which may bring the effective interest rate paid by the mortgagor down to as low as one percent—thus resulting in lower rents to the tenants. Eligible mortgagors include nonprofit and limited profit sponsors. Also, mortgage insurance is used to cover the financing of construction or rehabilitation. Almost a half million dwelling units are insured with a value of over $7 billion. New commitments will not be made under this program except when they cannot be accommodated under the Lower Income Housing Assistance (Section 8) program. Benefits are conditioned on need.

A

Authorization: Section 236 of the National Housing Act as amended in 1968, and as amended by the Housing and Community Development Act of 1974, 12 USC 1715(Z)-1.

Budget Code: 86-0139-0-1-604, 86-0148-0-1-604

Catalog Code: 14.103

FY77 Expenditure (est.)

$527 million

Represents the amount to be expended to liquidate contract authority.

PUBLIC LOW-INCOME HOUSING

Housing Production and Mortgage Credit, Housing Management, Department of Housing & Urban Development

Low-income families and elderly or disabled individuals are provided low-rent public housing that is decent, safe, and sanitary. Benefits are in kind, funded by project grants and direct loans to local public housing agencies for the purposes of acquisition (purchasing existing housing, procuring construction, letting contracts to private developers), subsidizing annual debt service payments, insuring adequate operation and maintenance, and modernization and expansion of facilities and services. There is no requirement for local matching; however, an indirect local contribution results from property tax abatements given local housing authorities. Benefits are conditioned on need.

A

Authorization: National Housing Act of 1937, as amended, PL75-412, 42 USC 1401-1435.

Budget Code: 86-0139-0-1-604, 86-0163-0-1-604, 86-0164-0-1-604, 86-4098-0-3-604

Catalog Code: 14.146, 14.147, 14.158

FY77 Expenditure (est.)

$1,112 million

About 50% of outlays represent operating subsidies; and over 10%, acquisition and modernization expenditures.

FARM LABOR HOUSING

Farmers Home Administration, Department of Agriculture

Domestic farm laborers and their families are provided decent, safe and sanitary low-rent housing and related facilities. Benefits are in kind, funded by 90-percent grants and by loans insured by the Rural Housing Insurance Fund. Both grants and loans may be made to nonprofit agencies and public bodies; only loans may be made to individual farmers and associations of farmers. About 400 dwelling units are provided for by grants annually, and about 700 by loans. Benefits are not directly conditioned on need.

B

Authorization: Sections 514 and 516 of the Housing Act of 1949, as amended, 42 USC 1484, 1486.

Budget Code: 12-2004-0-1-401, 12-4141-0-3-401

Catalog Code: 10.405

FY77 Expenditure (est.)

$7 million

Loan fund capital outlays and operating expenses in FY77 are to be more than offset by receipts, including sales and beneficial ownership certificates. Estimated FY77 loan commitments are $10 million; grant outlays, $7 million.

RURAL RENTAL HOUSING LOANS

Farmers Home Administration, Department of Agriculture

Low- and moderate-income families and senior citizens in rural areas are provided rental and cooperative housing (and related facilities) that they can afford. Benefits are in kind to the occupants, funded by favorable credit terms for the developer. Insured loans can be used to purchase, construct, improve or repair rental housing, and the loans are made to individual developers as well as to cooperatives and to nonprofit and public agencies. Eventual occupants pay 25 percent of the income as rent, but very low-income occupants pay only 15 percent. Loans covering some 27,000 units are to be made in 1977 in conjunction with subsidized housing assistance, and loans covering almost 5,000 units are to be made without such assistance. Benefits are conditioned on need.

B

Authorization: Sections 515 and 521 of the Housing Act of 1949, as amended, 42 USC 1485, 1490a.

Budget Code: 12-4141-0-3-401

Catalog Code: 10.415

FY77 Expenditure (est.)

-negative-

Loan fund capital outlays and operating expenses in FY77 are to be more than offset by receipts, including sales of beneficial ownership certificates. Estimated FY77 loan commitments are $545 million.

HOMEOWNERSHIP ASSISTANCE AND PAYMENTS

Housing Production and Mortgage Credit, Department of Housing & Urban Development

Lower-income families are provided new or substantially rehabilitated single-family houses or condominium units with annual mortgage payments equal to at least 20 percent of adjusted income. Benefits are in kind, funded by monthly interest subsidies to the mortgagee, on FHA insured loans, which bring the interest rate paid on pre-1976 mortgages down to as low as one percent, and on post-1976 mortgages to as low as five percent. Down payments are minimal, usually six percent of the acquisition cost. Almost a half million houses are insured, with a value of almost $9 billion. The average interest subsidy is about $1,010 annually per house. Approximately 100,000 commitments on homes are expected to be made this year, resulting in some $2.6 billion in reservations on $7.9 billion obligated, by court order, in 1976. Benefits are conditioned on need.

B

Authorization: Sections 235(i), (j) of the National Housing Act, as amended by PL90-448 and PL94-375, 12 USC 1715(b) and (z).

Budget Code: 86-0139-0-1-604, 86-0148-0-1-604

Catalog Code: 14.104, 14.105, 14.106

FY77 Expenditure (est.)

$148 million

Represents the amount to be expended to liquidate contract authority.

LOW TO MODERATE INCOME RURAL HOUSING LOANS

Farmers Home Administration, Department of Agriculture

Low- and moderate-income persons who own or will own land in rural areas are provided guaranteed or insured loans for the purchase of houses and/or building sites, as well as for the construction, repair or replacement of dwellings and essential farm buildings. Benefits are in the form of favorable credit terms and interest subsidies, funded by the Rural Housing Insurance Fund. Insured loans currently bear interest of eight percent, but low-income families may receive interest credits which reduce the effective interest rate paid to as low as one percent, depending on the size of loan, family size, and income. Low-income families are to receive 65,000 insured loans in 1977, totalling just over $1.5 billion in conjunction with subsidized housing assistance, and 7,500 insured loans, totalling $110 million without such assistance. Moderate-income families are to receive 65,000 insured or guaranteed loans totalling almost $1.5 billion without subsidized housing assistance. Benefits are conditioned on need.

B

Authorization: Section 502 of the Housing Act of 1949, as amended, 42 USC 1472, 1480; 7 USC 1933.

Budget Code: 12-4141-0-3-401

Catalog Code: 10.410

FY77 Expenditure (est.)

-negative-

Loan fund capital outlays and operating expenses in FY77 are to be more than offset by receipts, including sales of beneficial ownership certificates. Estimated FY77 loan commitments are $2.64 billion.

HOUSING REHABILITATION LOANS

Community Planning and Development, Department of Housing & Urban Development

Owners and tenants of residential and business property in urban renewal and federally assisted code enforcement areas are provided low-interest loans to rehabilitate such structures. Loans may be up to 20-year maturity. Benefits are in the form of favorable credit terms, funded by direct loans (from the Federal Rehabilitation Loan Fund) of up to $17,400 per dwelling unit. As many as 10,000 loans may be approved this year. Benefits are not conditioned on need.

C

Authorization: Section 312 of the Housing Act of 1964, as amended; PL85-560; 42 USC 1452.

Budget Code: 86-4036-0-3-451

Catalog Code: 14.220

FY77 Expenditure (est.)

$34 million

Loan fund capital outlays and operating expenses in FY77 are to be partially offset by receipts from loan repayments and interest revenue. Estimated FY77 loan commitments are $61 million.

RURAL SELF-HELP HOUSING TECHNICAL ASSISTANCE

Farmers Home Administration, Department of Agriculture

Low-income persons and their families are provided technical and supervisory assistance in carrying out mutual self-help projects of constructing housing in rural areas. Benefits are in kind, funded by project grants to public or private nonprofit agencies. No local matching is required. The project grants pay for administration and operation, as well as for training self-help group members and providing them with essential equipment such as power tools. Funds cannot be used for hiring construction personnel or for buying land or building materials. The average project grant is about $200,000. Benefits are conditioned on need.

C

Authorization: Section 523 of the Housing Act of 1949, as amended, 42 USC 1490c.

Budget Code: 12-2006-0-1-401

Catalog Code: 10.420

FY77 Expenditure (est.)

$6 million

Includes over 5% for project administration.

INDIAN HOUSING IMPROVEMENT

Bureau of Indian Affairs,
Department of Interior

Indians in need of financial assistance to help renovate or repair existing houses, or to build new houses where no other program will meet the need, are provided cash aid (frequently in conjunction with other Federal programs). Benefits are in cash for a restricted purpose, funded by project grants approved by the tribe. The average repair cost is about $3,100 and the average contribution toward a new home is $12,000. Approximately 400 new homes are started annually and about 8,000 are repaired or renovated (6,000 of which are also assisted by the Department of Housing and Urban Development). Benefits are conditioned on need.

B

Authorization: Snyder Act of 1921, PL67-85, 25 USC 13.

Budget Code: 14-2100-0-1-999

Catalog Code: 15.116

FY77 Expenditure (est.)

$14 million

INDIAN SANITATION FACILITIES

Health Services Administration, Department of Health, Education & Welfare

Sanitation facilities are constructed for Federal and tribal housing projects, as well as for existing homes near the project sites, for American Indian and Alaskan native families. Benefits are in kind; funding is for construction grants and contracts not requiring any matching by the tribe but an equitable contribution of labor or material in some instances. Approximately 11,000 families are provided sanitation facilities in the year. Benefits are not directly conditioned on need.

C

Authorization: PL83-568, Indian Sanitation Facilities Act; PL86-121, 42 USC 2004a; Indian Self-Determination Act, PL93-638, 25 USC 450.

Budget Code: 75-0391-0-1-554

Catalog Code: 13.229

FY77 Expenditure (est.)

$35 million

EMERGENCY ENERGY CONSERVATION SERVICES

Community Services Administration

Low-income persons and the near poor are provided a variety of services to lessen the impact of the high cost of energy and to reduce energy consumption. Services include consumer education, legal assistance, transportation assistance to services and jobs, home weatherization to minimize heat loss, and crisis intervention (grants, loans, fuel vouchers or stamps) to prevent utility shutoff or lack of fuel. Benefits are mainly in kind, funded by grants to community action agencies and other public and private nonprofit agencies. The local share requirement, 25 to 30 percent, is waived for crisis intervention. Benefits are conditioned on need.

B

Authorization: Section 222a(12) of the Community Services Act of 1974, PL93-644, 42 USC 2790.

Budget Code: 81-0500-0-1-999

Catalog Code: 49.014

FY77 Expenditure (est.)

$242 million

FHA MORTGAGE INSURANCE

Federal Housing Administration Fund, Department of Housing & Urban Development

Through more than 30 subprograms, different categories of home-buyers and renters are provided assistance to live in standard quality houses, condominiums, apartments, and mobile homes. Benefits are in the form of favorable credit and down payment terms on housing, funded by FHA's insuring of private lenders against losses on loans used to finance the purchase, repair, rehabilitation, or improvement of approved properties and dwelling units. About $10 billion of insurance will be written on 430,000 units this year, resulting in a total outstanding balance in force of some $90 billion in mortgage insurance. Benefits are not conditioned on need.

C

Authorization: Titles I and II of the National Housing Act of 1937, PL73-479, as amended, 12 USC 1703, 1709, 1713, 1715, 1745.

Budget Code: 86-4070-0-3-401

Catalog Code: 14.108-14.140, 14.142, 14.151-14.155

FY77 Expenditure (est.)

$647 million

FHA Fund capital outlays (acquisition of properties, defaults) and operating expenses in FY77 are to be partially offset by receipts from fees, premiums, property sales, and interest revenue. Estimated FY77 capital commitments are $1.03 billion.

VETERANS HOUSING — GUARANTEED AND INSURED LOANS

Department of Veterans Benefits, Veterans Administration

Non-dishonorably discharged veterans meeting active service requirements, those with service-connected disabilities, and unmarried widows and widowers of veterans whose deaths were service-connected, are provided guarantees or insurance on loans from private lenders to purchase, construct and/or improve homes and farms on which there are homes, to refinance mortgages on homes already owned, and to purchase mobile homes or improve lots for the placement of mobile homes. Benefits are in the form of favorable credit terms, financed from a revolving fund that provides for the expenses of settling guaranty claims. About 325,000 loans worth $10 billion are processed annually, as are 35,000 claims, acquisitions and repurchases on defaults and foreclosures. (Some $75 billion in guaranteed loans is outstanding.) Benefits are not conditioned on need.

C

Authorization: 38 USC 1810.

Budget Code: 36-4025-0-3-704

Catalog Code: 64.114, 64.119

FY77 Expenditure (est.)

$27 million

Loan guaranty fund capital outlays (acquisitions of property, defaults) and operating expenses in FY77 are almost entirely offset by receipts, including the sale of loans and properties, repayments, and interest revenue. Estimated FY77 capital commitments are $454 million.

VETERANS HOUSING — DIRECT LOANS

Department of Veterans Benefits, Veterans Administration

Non-dishonorably discharged veterans meeting active service requirements, those with service-connected disabilities, and unmarried widows and widowers of veterans whose deaths were service-connected, are provided direct loans to purchase, construct and/or improve homes and farms on which there are homes in rural areas and small towns where private capital is not generally available for VA guaranteed or insured loans. Benefits are in the form of favorable credit terms, financed from a revolving fund with loan amounts up to $33,000 for periods up to 30 years. Cash advances are also made on behalf of borrowers to protect the VA's interest, and these advances are added to the borrowers' unpaid loan balances. Approximately 2,700 loans are made annually, and the average loan is just over $20,000. Benefits are not conditioned on need.

C

Authorization: 38 USC 1811, as amended by PL94-324.

Budget Code: 36-4024-0-3-704

Catalog Code: 64.113, 64.118

FY77 Expenditure (est.)

-negative-

Loan fund capital outlays and operating costs in FY77 are to be more than offset by receipts, including loan sales, repayments and interest revenue. Estimated FY77 loan commitments are $75 million.

HEAD START

Office of Human Development, Department of Health, Education & Welfare

Preschool children from low-income families are provided comprehensive educational, health, nutritional, social, and related services in both full- and part-day programs, as well as in summer programs for children about to enter kindergarten, at community-based centers. Benefits are in kind, including social services for the family, and are funded by project grants to public or private nonprofit agencies. A 20-percent non-Federal share must be met in cash or in kind. About 350,000 preschool children are served annually in full-year, summer and experimental centers. Benefits are conditioned on need, and they include "hard" services (health care, meals, day care) as well as "softer" services.

B

Authorization: Title V, Part A of the Community Services Act of 1974, PL93-644, 42 USC 2921 *et seq.*

Budget Code: 75-1636-0-1-500

Catalog Code: 13.600

FY77 Expenditure (est.)

$486 million

LEGAL SERVICES FOR THE POOR

Legal Services Corporation

Legal assistance is provided to low-income persons in most types of non-criminal proceedings. (Legal services funds may not be used in support of political activity, demonstrations, strikes, nor in cases involving abortion, military desertion, school desegregation, and homosexual rights.) Benefits are in kind, funded by payment to the Corporation from general revenues for the salaries of staff lawyers and other expenses. The Corporation raises substantial additional funds on its own. Approximately 3,000 attorneys in 700 offices handle a million legal matters annually. Benefits are conditioned on need.

B

Authorization: Legal Services Corporation Act of 1974, PL93-355, as amended.

Budget Code: 20-0501-0-1-751

Catalog Code: none

FY77 Expenditure (est.)

$125 million

INDIAN SOCIAL SERVICES — COUNSELING

Bureau of Indian Affairs, Department of Interior

Advisory and counseling services are provided to the major part of the General Assistance and child welfare caseloads, as well as to other Indians residing on or near reservations who have family or social problems. Besides counseling and advice, liaison assistance with state and local agencies is provided to secure appropriate welfare services. Benefits are in kind, funded through the salaries and expenses of BIA social workers. No local matching is required. About 15,700 families, besides those on the welfare caseloads, receive services annually. Benefits are conditioned, in part, on need.

B

Authorization: Snyder Act of 1921, PL67-85, 25 USC 13.

Budget Code: 14-2100-0-1-452

Catalog Code: 15.132

FY77 Expenditure (est.)

$9 million

IV
PROGRAMS PROVIDING BENEFITS TO IMPROVE THE EARNINGS POTENTIAL OF THE INDIVIDUAL

FEDERAL EMPLOYMENT FOR DISADVANTAGED YOUTH

Civil Service Commission

Young people, aged 16 through 21, who need extra income to stay in school or to return to school after summer vacation are provided part-time jobs (up to 16 hours weekly) during the school year and/or full-time jobs during summer vacation in the Federal government. Benefits are in the form of cash compensation for work performed, funded by various accounts of participating Federal agencies. About 20,000 youths participate in the part-time, stay-in-school program monthly, and another 40,000 participate only in the minimum-wage summer program. Benefits are conditioned on need. This program, while compensating individuals for work, is a public employment program.

C

Authorization: Civil Service Act, PL89-554, 5 USC 3302.

Budget Code: none

Catalog Code: 27.003, 27.004

FY77 Expenditure (est.)

$105 million

Does not include administration costs which are provided for by each participating agency.

HIGHER EDUCATION WORK-STUDY

Office of Education, Department of Health, Education & Welfare

Part-time employment (up to 40 hours weekly) is provided in educational institutions or in the public interest, for undergraduate, graduate or professional students whose resources, including parental contributions, are determined to be inadequate to permit them to study at their institutions of higher education. Benefits are cash compensation, funded by means of an 80-percent reimbursement of student's earnings by the Federal government. Over 550,000 students are employed annually under this program. Benefits are conditioned on need; and, while the students are being compensated for work, this is a public employment program.

B

Authorization: Title IV, Part C of the Higher Education Act of 1965, PL89-329, 42 USC 2751-2752a; PL92-318.

Budget Code: 75-0293-0-1-502

Catalog Code: 13.463

FY77 Expenditure (est.)

$250 million

BASIC EDUCATIONAL OPPORTUNITY GRANTS

Office of Education, Department of Health, Education & Welfare

Undergraduate students, enrolled at least on a half-time basis at public or private, nonprofit institutions of postsecondary education, are provided financial aid not exceeding one half of their needs, for as many as four years. Grant levels are determined according to the cost of education, as well as on the basis of student and family contribution schedules. Benefits are in the form of cash, funded through the institutions acting as disbursing agents. About two million students receive grants averaging close to $900 yearly. Benefits are conditioned on need and satisfactory continuance of education.

A

Authorization: Section 411 of the Higher Education Amendments of 1972, PL92-318, 20 USC 1070a.

Budget Code: 75-0293-0-1-502

Catalog Code: 13.539

FY77 Expenditure (est.)

$1,461 million

INCENTIVE GRANTS FOR STATE SCHOLARSHIPS

Office of Education, Department of Health, Education & Welfare

Undergraduate students with substantial financial need are provided financial support for attendance on at least a half-time basis at postsecondary education institutions. Benefits are in the form of cash assistance, funded by formula grants to state scholarship or grant assistance agencies. The Federal funds are used for matching, up to $1,500 yearly for a full-time student's aid, the state's share of need-based aid. Over 170,000 needy students are assisted annually. Benefits are conditioned on need and on satisfactory continuance of education.

B

Authorization: Title IV, Part A of the Higher Education Act of 1965, PL89-329, as amended by PL92-318 and PL94-482.

Budget Code: 75-0293-0-1-502

Catalog Code: 13.548

FY77 Expenditure (est.)

$32 million

NATIONAL DIRECT STUDENT LOANS

Office of Education, Department of Health, Education & Welfare

Undergraduate and graduate students, with at least half the normal academic workload, are provided loans by their institutions, upon demonstrating financial need. Loan cancellation is allowed borrowers who enter military service in an area of hostilities or who teach in a poverty area, in a preschool program, or in a program for handicapped children. Such cancellations are reimbursed to the lending institution by the Federal government. Benefits are in the form of favorable credit terms, funded by grants to higher education institutions for establishing loan funds (10 percent of which must be locally raised) and by reimbursements to those funds for cancelled loans. Over 800,000 students receive loans amounting to $570,000,000 annually. Benefits are conditioned, in part, on need.

B

Authorization: Title IV, Part E of the Higher Education Act of 1965, PL89-329, 20 USC 1087aa-ff; Title II of the National Defense Education Act of 1958, PL85-864, 20 USC 421-429.

Budget Code: 75-0293-0-1-502

Catalog Code: 13.470, 13.471

FY77 Expenditure (est.)

$12 million

Represents amount required for loan cancellations. Institutional loan funds presently have sufficient balances.

HIGHER EDUCATION ACT INSURED LOANS

Office of Education,
Department of Health, Education & Welfare

Undergraduate and vocational students are provided low-interest, deferred loans of up to $2,500 a year, and graduate students up to $5,000 a year, to defray the cost of education. Any student whose adjusted family income is under $25,000 automatically qualifies for interest subsidies on loan amounts up to $2,500. Other students may also qualify, pursuant to institutional recommendations as to their loan amounts. Repayment begins 9 to 12 months after a student ceases to carry at least one half of a normal academic workload, but repayment may be additionally deferred for up to three years while a student is in the Armed Forces, VISTA or Peace Corps. Benefits are in the form of favorable credit terms and federally enabled loan guarantees, annually covering almost 800,000 loans (amounting to $1,275,000,000) to 420,000 students. No local matching is required. Benefits are conditioned, in part, on need.

B

Authorization: Title IV, Part B of the Higher Education Act of 1965, PL89-329, 20 USC 1071, as amended; and PL91-95, 20 USC 1078(a).

Budget Code: 75-0293-0-1-502, 75-4308-0-3-502

Catalog Code: 13.460

FY77 Expenditure (est.)

$484 million

Includes about $340 million in interest subsidies and $140 million in acquisition of defaults.

VETERANS DEPENDENTS EDUCATIONAL ASSISTANCE

Department of Veterans Benefits, Veterans Administration

Spouses, surviving spouses, sons and daughters of non-dishonorably discharged veterans whose deaths are service-connected or with permanent and total service-connected disabilities are provided financial assistance toward attaining an educational or vocational objective at an approved institution. Dependents are eligible for interest-bearing education loans of up to $1,500 per academic year, tutorial assistance allowances, and direct monthly payments, generally for no more than 45 months at $292 monthly for full-time students. Part-time educational efforts qualify for proportionate monthly subsistence payments. About 115,000 dependents receive direct payments that average about $2,000 yearly. Substantially fewer than 10,000 loans are made annually to dependents without sufficient funds to meet their expenses. Direct payments are not conditioned on need; loans are conditioned on need.

B

Authorization: 38 USC 1710, as amended by PL93-337, PL94-502.

Budget Code: 36-0137-0-1-702, 36-4118-0-3-702

Catalog Code: 64.117

FY77 Expenditure (est.)

$210 million

Estimated FY77 loan commitments are approximately $12 million.

178

VETERANS EDUCATIONAL ASSISTANCE

Department of Veterans Benefits, Veterans Administration

Non-dishonorably discharged veterans with at least 181 continuous days of active service, any part of which occurred after January, 1955, or such veterans discharged after that date because of a service-connected disability, are provided financial assistance toward attaining an educational or vocational objective at an approved institution. Veterans are eligible for interest-bearing education loans of up to $1,500 per academic year, work-study allowances, tutorial assistance allowances and direct monthly payments, generally for no more than 45 months and varying from $292 for a single veteran to $396 for a veteran with two dependents, and $24 monthly for each additional dependent. Part-time educational efforts qualify for proportionate monthly subsistence payments. Some two million veterans receive direct payments that average almost $2,000 yearly. Less than 10,000 loans are made annually to veterans without sufficient funds to meet their expenses. Direct payments are not conditioned on need; loans are conditioned on need.

B

Authorization: 38 USC 1621, 1652, 1661, 1686 as amended by PL93-337, PL94-502.

Budget Code: 36-0137-0-1-702, 36-4118-0-3-702

Catalog Code: 64.111, 64.120

FY77 Expenditure (est.)

$3,683 million

Estimated FY77 loan commitments are approximately $12 million.

EXCLUSION OF VETERANS EDUCATIONAL ASSISTANCE

Internal Revenue Service, Department of Treasury

Additional financial assistance is provided indirectly to individuals who receive educational assistance under the G.I. Bill during the year. Benefits are in the form of tax relief, funded by allowing the veterans (or their dependents or survivors) to exclude from consideration as income such assistance. (In fact, all benefits and services of the Veterans Administration are non-taxable.) Benefits are not conditioned on need.

B

Authorization: 38 USC 3101.

Budget Code: none

Catalog Code: none

FY77 Expenditure (est.)

$255 million

Represents estimated FY77 revenue loss. About 75% of such tax expenditures go to tax filers with adjusted gross incomes under $7,000; and 18%, to those between $7,000 and $15,000.

NURSING STUDENT LOANS

Health Resources Administration, Department of Health, Education & Welfare

Full- and half-time nursing students with limited financial resources, at schools that prepare students for practice as registered nurses, are provided long-term, low-interest loans of up to $2,500 yearly to cover educational costs. Benefits are in the form of favorable credit terms, funded by allocations to the schools for the purpose of capitalizing student loan funds. At least ten percent of each fund must be contributed by the school. Benefits are conditioned, in part, on need.

C

Authorization: Section 835 of the Public Health Service Act, PL78-410, as amended by PL94-63, 42 USC 297a.

Budget Code: 75-0712-0-1-550

Catalog Code: 13.364

FY77 Expenditure (est.)

$23 million

HEALTH PROFESSIONS — STUDENT LOANS

Health Resources Administration, Department of Health, Education & Welfare

Full-time students with limited financial resources, at schools of medicine, osteopathy, dentistry, optometry, podiatry, pharmacy and veterinary medicine, are provided long-term, low-interest loans of up to $3,500 yearly to cover the costs of tuition, fees, books, equipment and related expenses. Benefits are in the form of favorable credit terms, funded by allocations to the schools for the purpose of capitalizing student loan funds. Schools must contribute at least ten percent of funds on deposit. Approximately 16,000 students in 250 schools are assisted annually. Benefits are conditioned, in part, on need.

C

Authorization: Part C, Section 740 of the Public Health Service Act, PL78-410, as amended.

Budget Code: 75-0712-0-1-550

Catalog Code: 13.342

FY77 Expenditure (est.)

$20 million

EXEMPTION FOR CHILDREN WHO ARE OVER AGE 18 AND STUDENTS

Internal Revenue Service, Department of Treasury

Indirect financial assistance is provided to taxpayers supporting older children who are students. Benefits are in the form of tax relief, funded by allowing the taxpayers to continue claiming $750 personal exemptions for their children over the age of 18 who are full-time students. Such children may have their own earnings or other income, over $750 yearly, but they must rely on their parents for a majority of their support. (The children may also claim an exemption for themselves on their own tax returns, thus providing a double exemption.) Benefits are not conditioned on need.

C

Authorization: Section 151(e) of the Internal Revenue Code of 1954, as amended.

Budget Code: none

Catalog Code: none

FY77 Expenditure (est.)

$750 million

Represents estimated FY77 revenue loss. About 7% of such tax expenditures go to tax filers with adjusted gross incomes under $7,000; and 48%, to those between $7,000 and $15,000.

EXCLUSION OF SCHOLARSHIPS AND FELLOWSHIPS

Internal Revenue Service, Department of Treasury

Additional financial assistance is provided indirectly to individuals who are supported by scholarships or fellowships in pursuit of their studies. Benefits are in the form of tax relief, funded by allowing the individual to exclude from consideration as income the value of such support. The exclusion does not apply to any amount which may be construed as payment for teaching, research or similar services. Scholarships and fellowships for non-degree candidates are limited as to the excludable amount. Benefits are not conditioned on need.

C

Authorization: Section 117 of the Internal Revenue Code of 1954, as amended.

Budget Code: none

Catalog Code: none

FY77 Expenditure (est.)

$250 million

Represents estimated FY77 revenue loss. About 48% of such tax expenditures go to tax filers with adjusted gross incomes under $7,000; and 37%, to those between $7,000 and $15,000.

UPWARD BOUND

Office of Education, Department of Health, Education & Welfare

Children from low-income families and with inadequate secondary school preparation are provided academic instruction, career and academic counseling, guidance, and a $30 monthly stipend, to prepare them for placement in college. Benefits are in kind, primarily social services, and in cash, funded by grants to postsecondary education institutions, and public and private agencies. No local matching is required. Almost 50,000 students are aided each year by the program. Benefits are conditioned on need and on continuation of education.

B

Authorization: Title IV-A of the Higher Education Act of 1965, PL89-329, as amended by PL90-575, PL92-318, and PL94-482, 20 USC 1101.

Budget Code: 75-0293-0-1-502

Catalog Code: 13.492

FY77 Expenditure (est.)

$39 million

SPECIAL SERVICES FOR DISADVANTAGED STUDENTS

Office of Education, Department of Health, Education & Welfare

Counseling, tutoring, career guidance, placement, student personnel and other educational services are provided to low-income, physically handicapped and language handicapped students enrolled at, or accepted for enrollment by, institutions of postsecondary education. Benefits are in kind, funded by grants to the educational institutions. No local matching is required. Grants must be used specifically on the disadvantaged students and cannot duplicate services available under other programs. About 100,000 disadvantaged students receive services annually. Benefits are conditioned, in part, on need and on satisfactory continuation of education.

C

Authorization: Higher Education Amendment of 1968, PL90-575, 20 USC 1101; PL92-318; PL93-380, 20 USC 821; PL94-482.

Budget Code: 75-0293-0-1-502

Catalog Code: 13.482

FY77 Expenditure (est.)

$20 million

EDUCATIONAL OPPORTUNITY CENTERS

Office of Education,
Department of Health, Education & Welfare

Through community-based centers in low-income areas, residents are provided with information about financial and other assistance available for postsecondary education. Residents are assisted in preparing admissions and financial aid applications, and enrolled postsecondary students are provided tutoring and counseling services. Benefits are in kind, primarily in the form of social services, funded by grants to postsecondary education institutions, as well as to combinations of such institutions and public and private agencies. A 25-percent non-Federal share is required. Benefits are not directly conditioned on need.

C

Authorization: Section 417A and B of the Higher Education Act of 1965, PL89-329, as amended by PL92-318 and PL94-482.

Budget Code: 75-0293-0-1-502

Catalog Code: 13.543

FY77 Expenditure (est.)

$3 million

TALENT SEARCH

Office of Education,
Department of Health, Education & Welfare

Secondary school students, as well as high school and college dropouts, who are disadvantaged financially or culturally but possess exceptional potential for postsecondary education, are identified, encouraged to pursue their education, and assisted in gaining admission to, and financial aid for, postsecondary schools. (No instruction, tutoring, or financial aid is provided directly by this program.) Benefits are in kind, primarily in the form of social services, funded by grants to institutions of higher education, as well as to public and private agencies. No local matching is required. Almost 150,000 disadvantaged students are assisted annually. Benefits are conditioned, in part, on need.

C

Authorization: Higher Education Amendment of 1968, PL90-575, 20 USC 1101; PL92-318, PL94-482.

Budget Code: 75-0293-0-1-502

Catalog Code: 13.488

FY77 Expenditure (est.)

$5 million

COMPREHENSIVE MANPOWER AND TRAINING SERVICES

Employment and Training Administration, Department of Labor

Unemployed, underemployed and disadvantaged persons are provided training and manpower services through a variety of subprograms. Programs for special groups, such as migrant farm workers and Indians, are under national direction, while other programs are determined and administered by 400 state and local prime sponsors. Benefits are in kind, funded by formula grants to prime sponsors based on area income and unemployment data as well as previous grant levels. Typical programs include outreach, counseling, testing, work experience, vocational skills training (either in the classroom or on the job), remedial education, placement, and supportive services. A million enrollees are served annually. In most programs, benefits are conditioned, in part, on need.

B

Authorization: Titles I, II, and IIIA of the Comprehensive Employment and Training Act of 1973, PL93-203, as amended.

Budget Code: 16-0174-0-1-504

Catalog Code: 17.228, 17.230, 17.232, 17.234

FY77 Expenditure (est.)

$1,414 million

Includes 15% for project administration and other support.

EMPLOYMENT SERVICE

Employment and Training Administration, Department of Labor

Persons seeking employment are provided counseling, testing, and referral to jobs, appropriate training or other services through 2,400 local offices. Specialized services are provided veterans, disadvantaged persons, youth, older workers, the handicapped, and rural residents. Benefits are in kind, funded by formula grants to state employment security agencies. Over 14 million applications are processed annually, resulting in a million counseling sessions, a million tests administered and almost 5 million job placements. Benefits are not directly conditioned on need.

B

Authorization: The Wagner-Peyser Act of 1933, PL73-30, as amended, 29 USC 49-49n and 39 USC 338; Title IV, Section C of the Social Security Act of 1935, as amended, 42 USC 602 *et seq.* and 42 USC 1101 *et seq.*; PL93-508; PL93-618; PL93-203; PL93-112; PL94-567; PL94-45.

Budget Code: 16-0179-0-1-504

Catalog Code: 17.207

FY77 Expenditure (est.)

$614 million

INDIAN EMPLOYMENT ASSISTANCE

Bureau of Indian Affairs, Department of Interior

Indians residing on or near reservations are provided vocational training in approved schools, employment counseling, and job placement assistance. Vocational training must not exceed two years, and can include on-the-job training. Benefits are in kind, funded by project grants, ranging from $800 to $5,500 yearly, made directly to Indian applicants. Over 17,000 Indians are assisted annually, at an average cost of $1,700 each. Benefits are not directly conditioned on need.

B

Authorization: Snyder Act of 1921, PL67-85, 25 USC 13; Indian Adult Vocational Training Act of 1956, PL84-959, 25 USC 309.

Budget Code: 14-2100-0-1-999

Catalog Code: 15.108

FY77 Expenditure (est.)

$36 million

MANAGEMENT ASSISTANCE TO DISADVANTAGED BUSINESSMEN

Small Business Administration

Economically or socially disadvantaged businessmen and potential businessmen, or those located in areas with a high concentration of unemployment, are provided management and technical assistance in planning, research, new business opportunities, legal, business and related services. Benefits are in kind, funded by project grants to public and private organizations. No local contribution is required. Approximately 4,500 small businessmen are served annually. Benefits are conditioned, in part, on need.

C

Authorization: Sections 7(i) and (j) of the Small Business Act, PL85-536, as amended, 15 USC 636(I) and (J).

Budget Code: 73-0100-0-1-403

Catalog Code: 59.007

FY77 Expenditure (est.)

$7 million

JOB CORPS

Employment and Training Administration, Department of Labor

Low-income youths, aged 14 to 21, are provided intensive educational and vocational training in a residential setting. Corps members also receive room and board, medical and dental care, work clothing, a monthly $30 living allowance initially, rising to over $50 subsequently, a readjustment allowance of $50 monthly for satisfactory service, as well as spouse and dependents allotments of up to $50 monthly. Benefits are in kind and in cash, funded by project grants to government agencies and private organizations. No local funding is required. Some 45,000 youths are trained, each for up to two years, at an average cost of $3,500 per year. Benefits are conditioned on need.

B

Authorization: Title IV of the Comprehensive Employment and Training Act of 1973, as amended, PL93-203, PL93-567, 29 USC 801 *et seq.*

Budget Code: 16-0174-0-1-504

Catalog Code: 17.211

FY77 Expenditure (est.)

$230 million

WORK INCENTIVE PROGRAM

Social and Rehabilitation Service, Department of Health, Education & Welfare and Employment and Training Administration, Department of Labor

Employable recipients of Aid to Families with Dependent Children (AFDC and AFDC-UF) are provided cash incentives, as well as manpower, employment and social services, to enable them to become self-supporting. Children under 16 or in school are exempt, as are disabled recipients and those required in the home for their care or for the care of preschool children. Non-exempt recipients may be provided assessment, testing, counseling, educational remediation, training, work experience and job placement (by the Department of Labor), as well as medical examinations and services, child care, transportation and relocation expenses (by the Department of Health, Education and Welfare). A $30 monthly stipend is provided, and approximately one third of net monthly earnings is disregarded as income upon placement in a job. Benefits are in cash and in services funded by 90-percent formula grants to state employment services and welfare agencies. About a half million recipients receive services each year, and as many as 200,000 may be placed in jobs. Benefits are conditioned on need.

A

Authorization: Social Security Act, as amended by PL90-248, PL92-178, and PL92-223, 42 USC 602, 630.

Budget Code: 75-0576-0-1-504

Catalog Code: 13.748, 17.226

FY77 Expenditure (est.)

$365 million

REHABILITATION SERVICES AND FACILITIES — BASIC SUPPORT

Office of Human Development, Department of Health, Education & Welfare

Persons with mental and physical handicaps, with an emphasis on the more severely disabled, are provided vocational rehabilitation services, including diagnosis and evaluation, counseling, training and employment services, assistance in paying for medical care and prosthetic/orthopedic devices, maintenance during rehabilitation, transportation, tools, equipment and supplies, reader services for the blind, interpreter services for the deaf, and small business opportunities. Benefits are mainly in kind, funded by formula grants to state vocational rehabilitation agencies which provide or purchase necessary services. Some state matching is required. More than one and a half million persons (including disabled recipients of public assistance) receive services annually; over 310,000 are rehabilitated. Benefits are not directly conditioned on need.

B

Authorization: Rehabilitation Act of 1973, PL93-112, as amended by PL93-516, PL94-230, 29 USC 701 *et seq.*

Budget Code: 75-1636-0-1-500

Catalog Code: 13.624

FY77 Expenditure (est.)

$733 million

VOCATIONAL REHABILITATION FOR DISABLED VETERANS

Department of Veterans Benefits, Veterans Administration

Non-dishonorably discharged veterans with service-connected, compensable disabilities are provided payments to cover the full cost of vocational rehabilitation (tuition, books, fees, supplies), monthly subsistence payments during training and for two months thereafter, and small, non-interest-bearing loans. Benefits are principally in the form of cash, funded by direct payments. Monthly subsistence payments are in addition to any disability compensation; and, for full-time attendance, they range from $226 for a single veteran to $329 for a veteran with two dependents and $24 for each additional dependent. Over 30,000 disabled veterans receive vocational rehabilitation payments annually, at an average total cost of almost $3,200, and almost 5,000 receive loans of up to $200. Benefits are not directly conditioned on need.

B

Authorization: 38 USC 1502, as amended by PL94-502.

Budget Code: 36-0137-0-1-702, 36-4114-0-3-702
Catalog Code: 64.116

FY77 Expenditure (est.)

$104 million

AUTOMOBILES AND ADAPTIVE EQUIPMENT — DISABLED VETERANS

Department of Veterans Benefits, Veterans Administration

Non-dishonorably discharged veterans of World War II and thereafter who incurred the loss, or permanent loss of use, of hand or foot, or impairment of vision of both eyes, are provided financial aid toward the purchase of an automobile or other conveyance (one time only, not to exceed $3,300), of necessary adaptive equipment for operating the vehicle, and of subsequent repair, replacement or reinstallation of the adaptive equipment. Benefits are in the form of cash, funded by direct Federal payment, restricted for a specific use, to the disabled veteran. Approximately 2,000 automobiles and other conveyances are purchased annually, and about 12,600 items of adaptive equipment are installed, repaired or replaced. Active service personnel also utilize this program. Benefits are not directly conditioned on need.

C

Authorization: 38 USC Chapter 39, as amended by PL94-433.

Budget Code: 36-0137-0-1-702

Catalog Code: 64.100

FY77 Expenditure (est.)

$14 million

VOCATIONAL REHABILITATION FOR SOCIAL SECURITY BENEFICIARIES

Office of Human Development, Department of Health, Education & Welfare

Selected disabled beneficiaries of old-age and survivors insurance, as well as disability insurance, are provided the full range of vocational rehabilitation services authorized by the Rehabilitation Act of 1973, in the expectation that savings will accrue to the Social Security trust funds as a result of the beneficiaries' return to gainful employment. Benefits are in kind, funded by direct payments into state-held trust funds, used to purchase the necessary services. Over 15,000 beneficiaries are rehabilitated annually. Benefits are not directly conditioned on need.

B

Authorization: Section 222(d) of the Social Security Act, as amended by PL89-97, 42 USC 422 (D).

Budget Code: 20-8006-0-7-601, 20-8007-0-7-601

Catalog Code: 13.625

FY77 Expenditure (est.)

$93 million

LOCAL PUBLIC WORKS EMPLOYMENT PROGRAM

Economic Development Administration, Department of Commerce

Unemployed persons are indirectly provided expanded job opportunities by stimulation of construction and construction-related activities on state and local government projects. Benefits are in the form of cash compensation for work performed, funded by means of 100-percent formula grants which take into account both the numbers of unemployed and the rate of unemployment of the states and localities. Construction must be initiated within 90 days of grant award. Benefits are not conditioned on need.

B

Authorization: Title I of the Public Works Employment Act of 1976, PL94-369, 42 USC 6701.

Budget Code: 13-2052-0-1-452

Catalog Code: none

FY77 Expenditure (est.)

$520 million

Represents FY77 actual outlays, of the total $6 billion obligated during FY77.

ECONOMIC DEVELOPMENT — PUBLIC WORKS

Economic Development Administration, Department of Commerce

Unemployed, underemployed and low-income persons are indirectly provided expanded job opportunities through the construction of public facilities, industrial parks, railroad sidings and spurs, access roads, water and sewer systems, flood control projects, etc., that encourage economic growth in depressed areas. Benefits are in the form of cash compensation for work performed, funded by project grants and direct loans to states, localities, and private or public nonprofit organizations. Grants generally require 20 percent to 50 percent local matching, and loans may be up to 40 years at low interest (but there are very few loan transactions). Benefits are not conditioned on need.

C

Authorization: Titles, I, II and IV of the Public Works and Economic Development Act of 1965, PL89-136, as amended by PL90-103, PL91-123, PL91-304, PL92-65, PL93-46, and PL93-423, 42 USC 3131, 3132, 3135, 3141, 3153, 3171, 3211.

Budget Code: 13-2050-0-1-452

Catalog Code: 11.300, 11.304, 11.308

FY77 Expenditure (est.)

$171 million

COMMUNITY ECONOMIC DEVELOPMENT

Community Services Administration

Residents of low-income areas are indirectly provided increased employment and business opportunities through the promotion of community-based economic development. Benefits are in kind, funded by 90-percent grants to locally controlled, nonprofit community development corporations which, in partnership with established businesses, undertake a variety of investment ventures in their areas. Approximately 20 community corporations are funded annually. Benefits are not directly conditioned on need.

C

Authorization: Economic Opportunity Act of 1964, as amended by the Community Services Act of 1974, Title VII of PL93-644, 42 USC 2981b.

Budget Code: 81-0500-0-1-999

Catalog Code: 49.011

FY77 Expenditure (est.)

$50 million

COMMUNITY ACTION

Community Services Administration

Low-income persons are provided a wide variety of services, planned and coordinated with local initiative by a community action (anti-poverty) agency, with the aim both of reducing poverty and its effects and of promoting self-determination. Services range from community organization and recreation to job development, training, placement and direct employment, to medical and dental care, emergency financial assistance, and housing. Benefits are largely in kind, funded by grants to 881 community action agencies, which must come up with 30 to 40 percent matching funds. Benefits frequently represent an enrichment of traditional public services adapted for a special subpopulation. Benefits are conditioned, in part, on need.

C

Authorization: Economic Opportunity Act of 1964, as amended by the Community Services Act of 1974, Title II of PL93-644, 42 USC 2790 *et seq.*

Budget Code: 81-0500-0-1-999

Catalog Code: 49.002

FY77 Expenditure (est.)

$346 million

VOLUNTEERS IN SERVICE TO AMERICA

ACTION

Community organizations in low-income areas are assisted in efforts to eliminate poverty and its effects through the provision of full-time trained volunteers who then live in the community. Depending on a community's needs and a volunteer's training and education, services provided relate to health, education, community development, housing, social services and economic development. Benefits are thus in kind, funded by means of the subsistence allowances paid the volunteers. No local funding is required. Over 4,000 volunteers are working with some 500 sponsoring organizations; a majority of the volunteers are now recruited from the community in which they work. Benefits are not directly conditioned on need.

B

Authorization: Domestic Volunteer Service Act of 1973, PL93-113.

Budget Code: 44-0103-0-1-451

Catalog Code: 72.003

FY77 Expenditure (est.)

$23 million

Includes over 20% for administration and other support.

INDIAN CREDIT PROGRAM

Bureau of Indian Affairs,
Department of Interior

Indians, Alaskan natives, and Indian organizations are provided assistance in obtaining financing for purposes that will promote the economic development of their reservations, including industry, agriculture, housing, education and for re-lending by the tribe itself. Financing at reasonable terms must not be available from other sources. Benefits are in the form of cash (40-percent or $50,000 grants for establishing economic enterprises) and favorable credit terms (low-interest loans, loan guarantees and insurance, interest subsidies). Benefits are not directly conditioned on need.

C

Authorization: Section 10 of the Indian Reorganization Act of 1934, PL73-383, 25 USC 470; Indian Financing Act of 1974, PL93-262, 25 USC 1451.

Budget Code: 14-2100-0-1-999, 14-4409-0-3-452, 14-4410-0-3-452

Catalog Code: 15.124

FY77 Expenditure (est.)

$18 million

Loan fund capital outlays (acquisition of loans, defaults) and operating expenses in FY77 are to be partially offset by receipts from repayments, premiums and interest revenues. Estimated FY77 capital commitments are $22 million; grant outlays, $6 million.

NATIVE AMERICAN PROGRAMS

Office of Human Development, Department of Health, Education & Welfare

American Indians and native Hawaiians and Alaskans are provided a variety of services to promote self-determination, self-sufficiency, community development, and to fill in the gaps left by other programs. Benefits are in kind, including manpower training and employment, housing, food, medical and social services, funded by project grants to tribal governing bodies and public and nonprofit private agencies. Generally a 20-percent local contribution is required. Over a half million native Americans benefit annually, including 150,000 in urban organizations in 36 states. Eighty percent of beneficiaries are low-income. Benefits are not directly conditioned on need.

C

Authorization: Title VIII of the Community Service Act of 1974, PL93-644, 42 USC 2991 *et seq.*

Budget Code: 75-1636-0-1-500

Catalog Code: 13.612

FY77 Expenditure (est.)

$42 million

APPENDIX

CONSOLIDATED LIST OF PROGRAMS
AND OUTLAYS BY AGENCY

	Page	$ Millions
ACTION		
Foster Grandparent Program	35	40
Senior Companion Program	36	9
Volunteers in Service to America	203	23
Total		72
AGRICULTURE, DEPARTMENT OF		
Agricultural Stabilization and Conservation Service		
Cotton Production Stabilization Payments	100	108
Dairy and Beekeeper Indemnity Payments	99	4
Federal Crop Insurance	96	67
Feed Grain Production Stabilization Payments	101	228
Rice Production Stabilization Payments	102	135
Wheat Production Stabilization Payments	103	111
Wool and Mohair Payments	104	8
		661
Farmers Home Administration		
Emergency Loans	95	0
Farm Labor Housing	156	7
Farm Operating Loans	98	0
Farm Ownership Loans	115	0
Low to Moderate Income Rural Housing Loans	159	0
Rural Rental Housing Loans	157	0
Rural Self-Help Housing Technical Assistance	161	6
Very Low-Income Housing Repair Loans	70	5
		18
Food and Nutrition Service		
Child Care Food Program	150	115
Food Donations	145	28
Food Stamps	152	5,474
National School Lunch Program	147	2,204

	Page	$ Millions
School Breakfast Program	148	191
School Milk Program	146	177
Special Supplemental Food Program (WIC)	144	248
Summer Food Program	149	195
		8,632
Total		9,311

CIVIL SERVICE COMMISSION

Civil Service Disability Pensions	42	1,694
Civil Service Retirement Pensions	31	6,370
Civil Service Survivors Pensions	58	1,205
Federal Employment for Disadvantaged Youth	172	105
Retired Federal Employees Health Benefits	65	433
Total		9,807

COMMERCE, DEPARTMENT OF
Economic Development Administration

Economic Adjustment Assistance	94	30
Economic Development—Public Works	200	171
Local Public Works Employment Program	199	520
Total		721

COMMUNITY SERVICES ADMINISTRATION

Community Action	202	346
Community Economic Development	201	50
Community Food and Nutrition	151	29
Emergency Energy Conservation Services	164	242
Senior Opportunities and Services	34	11
Total		678

DEFENSE, DEPARTMENT OF

Military Disability Retirement	45	980
Military Nondisability Retirement	32	7,233
Military Survivors Benefits	59	120
Total		8,333

HEALTH, EDUCATION AND WELFARE, DEPARTMENT OF
Alcohol, Drug Abuse, and Mental Health Administration

Alcohol Community Service Programs	135	56
Community Mental Health Centers	136	79
Comprehensive Services Support	132	132

	Page	$ Millions
Drug Abuse Community Service Programs	133	159
Mental Health—Children's Services	131	18
		444
Health Resources Administration		
Health Professions — Student Loans	182	20
Nursing Student Loans	181	23
		43
Health Services Administration		
Community Health Centers	137	229
Comprehensive Public Health Services—		
Formula Grants	142	95
Crippled Children's Services	128	98
Family Planning Projects	129	121
Health Maintenance Organization Development	141	39
Indian Health Services	139	245
Indian Sanitation Facilities	163	35
Maternal and Child Health Services	130	241
Migrant Health Grants	140	32
National Health Service Corps	138	26
		1,161
Office of Education		
Basic Educational Opportunity Grants	174	1,461
Educational Opportunity Centers	187	3
Higher Education Act Insured Loans	177	484
Higher Education Work-Study	173	250
Incentive Grants for State Scholarships	175	32
National Direct Student Loans	176	12
Special Services for Disadvantaged Students	186	20
Talent Search	188	5
Upward Bound	185	39
		2,306
Office of Human Development		
Developmental Disabilities—Basic Support	83	32
Head Start	168	468
Native American Programs	205	42
Nutrition Programs for the Elderly	66	209
Rehabilitation Services and Facilities—		
Basic Support	195	733
State and Community Planning and Services		
for the Aging	62	140

	Page	$ Millions
Vocational Rehabilitation for Social Security		
Beneficiaries	198	93
		1,717
Social and Rehabilitation Service		
Aid to the Aged, Blind and Disabled	22	5
Aid to Families with Dependent Children	56	5,718
Aid to Families with Dependent Children—		
Unemployed Father	86	400
Cuban Refugee Assistance	120	68
Emergency Assistance to Needy Families with		
Children	118	60
Indochinese Refugee Assistance	119	95
Medical Assistance (Medicaid)	60	9,859
Social Services	61	2,645
Work Incentive Program	194	365
		19,215
Social Security Administration		
Disabled Coal Mine Workers Benefits and		
Compensation	43	935
Medicare—Hospital Insurance	64	15,314
Medicare—Supplementary Medical Insurance	63	6,330
Social Security—Disability Insurance	37	11,625
Social Security—Retirement Insurance	27	52,364
Social Security—Survivors Insurance	52	18,888
Special Benefits for Persons Age 72 and Over	26	236
Supplemental Security Income	20	5,299
		110,991
Total		135,877

HOUSING AND URBAN DEVELOPMENT, DEPARTMENT OF

	Page	$ Millions
Housing for the Elderly and Handicapped	68	262
Community Planning and Development		
Housing Rehabilitation Loans	160	34
Federal Disaster Assistance Administration		
Disaster Assistance	124	387
Federal Housing Administration Fund		
FHA Mortgage Insurance	165	647

Appendix

	Page	$ Millions
Federal Insurance Administration		
Crime/Riot Insurance	97	2
Flood Insurance	126	178
		180
Housing Production and Mortgage Credit		
Homeownership Assistance and Payments	158	148
Lower Income Housing Assistance Payments	153	362
Public Low-Income Housing	155	1,112
Rent Supplements	69	245
Rental Housing Assistance and Payments	154	527
		2,394
Total		3,904
INTERIOR, DEPARTMENT OF THE		
Bureau of Indian Affairs		
Indian Credit Program	204	18
Indian Employment Assistance	191	36
Indian General Assistance	121	64
Indian Housing Improvement	162	14
Indian Social Services—Counseling	170	9
Total		141
LABOR, DEPARTMENT OF		
Bureau of International Labor Affairs		
Trade Adjustment Assistance - Workers	93	254
Employment Standards Administration		
Disabled Coal Mine Workers Benefits and Compensation	43	*
Federal Employees Compensation Benefits	48	589
Longshoremen's and Harbor Workers' Compensation	47	6
		595
Employment and Training Administration		
Comprehensive Manpower and Training Services	189	1,414
Employment Service	190	614
Federal-State Unemployment Insurance	87	13,490
Job Corps	193	230

* See listing under HEW, Social Security Administration for program outlays.

	Page	$ Millions
Public Service Employment	113	3,159
Senior Community Service Employment	33	74
Special Unemployment Assistance	92	691
Summer Youth Employment	116	595
Unemployment Compensation for Federal		
Civilian Employees and Ex-Servicemen	89	712
Work Incentive Program	194	†
		20,979
	Total	21,828

LEGAL SERVICES CORPORATION

Legal Services for the Poor	Total 169	125

RAILROAD RETIREMENT BOARD

Railroad Disability Insurance	38	551
Railroad Retirement Insurance	29	2,250
Railroad Survivors Insurance	53	1,026
Railroad Unemployment Insurance	88	183
	Total	4,010

SMALL BUSINESS ADMINISTRATION

Economic Opportunity Loans	114	50
Handicapped Assistance Loans	51	13
Management Assistance to Disadvantaged		
Businessmen	192	7
Physical Disaster Loans	125	86
	Total	156

TRANSPORTATION, DEPARTMENT OF
  Coast Guard

Military Disability Retirement	45	‡
Military Nondisability Retirement	32	‡
Military Survivors Benefits	59	‡

TREASURY, DEPARTMENT OF THE
  Internal Revenue Service

Additional Exemption for the Aged	24	1,220
Additional Exemption for the Blind	23	20

† See listing under HEW, Social and Rehabilitation Service for program outlays.
‡ See listing under Department of Defense for program outlays.

Appendix

	Page	$ Millions
Credit for Child and Dependent Care Expenses	107	840
Credit for the Elderly	25	495
Deductibility of Casualty Losses	127	345
Deductibility of Medical Expenses	143	2,585
Earned Income Credit	105	1,070
Excess of Percentage Standard Deduction Over Low-Income Allowance	106	1,285
Exclusion from Capital Gains on Home Sales by the Elderly	67	40
Exclusion of Employer Contributions to Accident Insurance Premiums	111	70
Exclusion of Employer Contributions to Group Term Life Insurance Premiums	109	800
Exclusion of Employer Contributions to Medical Insurance Premiums	112	5,195
Exclusion of Employer Contributions to Pension and Profit-Sharing Plans	110	8,715
Exclusion of Employer Contributions to Supplementary Unemployment Insurance Trusts	91	10
Exclusion of Employer-Furnished Meals and Lodging	108	330
Exclusion of Interest on Life Insurance Savings	123	1,815
Exclusion of Military Disability Pensions	46	105
Exclusion of Public Assistance Benefits	21	100
Exclusion of Railroad Retirement Benefits	30	200
Exclusion of Scholarships and Fellowships	184	250
Exclusion of Sick Pay for the Disabled	50	50
Exclusion of Social Security Benefits	28	4,240
Exclusion of Special Benefits for Disabled Coal Miners	44	50
Exclusion of Unemployment Insurance Benefits	90	2,745
Exclusion of Veterans Educational Assistance	180	255
Exclusion of Veterans Pensions and Disability Compensation	41	685
Exclusion of Worker's Compensation Benefits	49	705
Exemption for Children Who Are Over Age 18 and Students	183	750
Total		34,970

	Page	$ Millions
VETERANS ADMINISTRATION		
Department of Medicine and Surgery		
Blind Veterans Rehabilitation Centers	78	3
Civilian Health and Medical Program—VA	75	29
Community Nursing Home Care	80	75
Veterans Contract Hospitalization	73	55
Veterans Domiciliary Care	81	69
Veterans Grants for State Home Care	82	36
Veterans Hospitalization	72	2,862
Veterans Nursing Home Care	79	147
Veterans Outpatient Care	74	872
Veterans Prescription Service	76	12
Veterans Prosthetic Appliances	77	50
Veterans Rehabilitation—Alcohol and Drug Dependence	134	107
		4,317
Department of Veterans Benefits		
Automobiles and Adaptive Equipment—Disabled Veterans	197	14
Burial Allowance for Veterans	57	150
Specially Adapted Housing for Disabled Veterans	71	14
Survivors Compensation for Service-Connected Deaths	54	1,067
Veterans Compensation for Service-Connected Disabilities	39	4,796
Veterans Dependents Educational Assistance	178	210
Veterans Educational Assistance	179	3,683
Veterans Housing—Direct Loans	167	0
Veterans Housing—Guaranteed and Insured Loans	166	27
Veterans Life Insurance	122	648
Veterans Pensions for Non-Service-Connected Disabilities	40	1,870
Veterans Survivors Pensions	55	1,322
Vocational Rehabilitation for Disabled Veterans	196	104
		13,905
Total		18,222
GRAND TOTAL OF ALL PROGRAM OUTLAYS		**248,155**

Authors' Note: Programs reorganized in 1977 are listed under the Federal agency or department under which they appear in the proposed 1978 Budget.

ALPHABETICAL INDEX
BY PROGRAM